To River's End

Daniel Robison

Cover design: Amelia Stark

ISBN: 9798492872953

For my sons, Isaac and Judah

CONTENTS

INTRODUCTION

The St. Johns River.

You can find the maps at any old marina from Okeechobee to Jacksonville. Unfolding one, you'll likely behold a pretty blue ribbon, bulging here and there with occasional splotches of lakes against a pleasant green background. Chances are these maps will be littered with all kinds of coordinates and depth charts, and with official, archived names for practically every slough and bend, giving the impression that everything to know about this River has been figured out and laid bare with scientific precision. Casually looking at these maps, you might be tempted to believe that this River has been stripped of all its wildness and mystery...that it has been tamed. But there is an old proverb that holds true here: Just because you've got it mapped don't mean you've got it licked! I think we would do well to mind this—in fact, maybe the whole story that follows is a case in point of its truthfulness.

The St. Johns River has been intricately woven into my life for many years now, and I can personally testify that both its wildness and its mystery are still very real. This River creates its own world; it has a rhythm, a pulse, a power that maps and charts cannot tell. A quick day ride roaring by in a motorboat won't reveal this River to you. You've got to slow down, quiet down, and humble yourself to move at its pace—to be a guest. For those who do, there still remains a chance to be changed by its power.

Now, I am not a well-known man; I am not exceptionally strong or brave, and I am not exceptionally smart—I am no one of consequence, really. Nevertheless, I believe I have a story about this River that is worth telling. It is a journey I will never forget, and as I now have boys of my own who are coming of age, one I feel compelled to share.

In the pages that follow, very little effort has been taken to gather the history of the places mentioned or to research the changes they have undergone since these events took place—this is intentional. My purpose in writing this book is not to give the reader an extensive history of the St. Johns River, but rather to share a brief moment in that history. I have also tried to capture the impressions I had when I was actually there, though in the years since I have gained further knowledge that could allow me to be more specific about some things. Where I have found actual errors in my original account, I have endeavored to render them more truthful, but where there is mystery and wonder, I have been content to leave it, even if it is at the expense of a little precision here and there.

-D.R.

THE RIVER'S WOMB

A rush of adrenaline had me awake and off the couch with the first strike of the alarm: 3:00 AM, March 16, 2009. It was time. I steadied myself against the music room piano for a moment, rubbing the glaze from my eyes, then grabbed my last minute necessities. Everything else had already been stashed in Jay's truck the night before.

The sharp scent of ash from the old stone fireplace mingled with freshly brewed coffee as I quietly made my way into the living room. The muffled song of crickets droned outside, a bit softer than last night. Lazy slivers from a gibbous moon glowed dully on the water just a few hundred yards beyond the sliding glass door. My own slim frame reflected against it: bare feet, short dark beard, glasses—it was the same reflection I always saw...and yet, somehow, it was different this time. Was I really doing this?

A quick creak split the stillness of the sleepy house, and I spun around to see Jay maneuvering gingerly down the stairs, not wanting to wake the family. He reached the bottom, raking fingers through his peppered beard and straightening his glasses.

"You ready?" he whispered.

I nodded, and grabbed my old wide brimmed canoeing hat from the chair. At the same time David stumbled out from his room, sporting an identical one over his unruly mop of blond hair. He had never been a morning person, even with a normal wake-up time; at that early hour, I was surprised he had gotten up on his own at all! He was groggy and unsteady on his feet, wearing the same tank top and ragged cargo shorts he had been sleeping in, and had just barely made it into his pair of boots which were dragging their untied laces behind them.

"Alright," he sniffed, rubbing the scruff on his chin, and broke into a drowsy smile, "let's do this!"

We were met with the damp, rich scent of earth and hyacinth as we walked out into the cool night. There was only a slight breeze creeping up from the water, but I was still so fresh from sleep that it seemed icy, and I held back a shiver as we made our way to the truck. The bows of Old Orange and New Blue—our kayaks for the trip—hung conspicuously far beyond the tailgate, lashed down securely to a bed extender.

Old Orange was a Wilderness Systems Pamlico 145t which Jay had bought many years earlier. She was, as our endearing name suggested, beginning to show her age a little. Scuff marks peppered her hull along with a couple of deeper gouges, and the fabric seats were faded and threadbare in places, but I loved that boat. She had gone with me on the very first long-distance trip I ever took on the River, and had faithfully borne me over many, many miles since. It only seemed right that I should be the one to take her. New Blue, the Wilderness Systems Pungo 140 that Jay had just recently purchased, would serve as David's boat.

We had carefully organized all our food in the drybags in the backseat, and as I opened the door, the tantalizing scents of nuts, grains, chips, chocolates, dried meats, and fruits swept around me so thick that my mouth tingled. I settled in the back, the heat of my own body quickly overpowering the chill of the stiff leather seat. David took the front passenger seat as Jay adjusted himself behind the wheel.

"This is it," David observed, buckling in. The engine came to life. The headlights blazed out, suddenly exposing the sleeping woods beyond, and we began our adventure, crunching down the narrow gravel road into the night.

This trip had really been many years in the making; you might even say it began when I got to pilot my first canoe at fifteen. There was something that clicked in me then, something that stayed with me long after I went home—a yearning for muddy banks, the gurgling of the current fighting at my bow, the smell of a lazy breeze sighing over cool water. In those early days, my friends and I explored all over the St. Johns River from Puzzle Lake to just south of Lake George, often supplied with nothing but a change of clothes, a bottle of water, and a bag of whatever snacks we could find in the pantry. Sometimes we would be out in the wilderness for days at a time, learning to read the shoreline, push our limits, and strengthen our wills. For us, the River became more than water; every time we pushed off from shore, we were traveling into a different reality that touched the mythical. Its watery way was a limitless frontier of pathless places, new discoveries, and hidden treasures.

We faced blazing Florida summers with their merciless insects and suffocating heat; we never really stopped sweating from the moment we left home until the moment we got back! We explored old logging canals left from the late 1800's, ancient cypress forests, Timucuan shell mounds—every bend seemed to hold new adventures. We got lost, nearly got ourselves sunk by alligators during a couple particular night runs, and passed out from heatstroke once on Lake Monroe...but the River kept calling us back.

Over the years, my friends and I paddled hundreds of miles, but always stayed within the River's middle basin. We had often talked about exploring farther south or north of our home base in Central Florida, but nothing had ever come of our plans until now. Things had changed when, last December, I had read a newspaper article about Keith Leggette and Seth Dent, two kayakers who had set the first known record for the fastest navigation of the entire St. Johns River: *eleven days*. I had just turned 23 at the time. I was a recent college graduate, and was set to marry my fiancée, Nicole, in June of that coming year; I was in a transitional time, and my schedule was incredibly flexible. Even before I had finished reading the article I knew I had to do it.

I pored over all the maps and satellite photos of the River that I could find, familiarizing myself with every lake and every bend. The number of factors to take into account seemed overwhelming at first, but my determination held out, and after several weeks I had put together a rough plan that would allow the journey to be completed in nine days—an ambitious two days faster than the record set by Keith and Seth. It looked great...on paper. Carrying it out would be the tricky part.

Out of all the guys I trusted, David had been the only one willing to make the time commitment for such a trip. He was only nineteen, but despite his age he was an experienced kayaker, and had fought with me through wind and waves, cold and heat, swamps and lakes. He was so excited when I told him about my idea that he resolved, right then and there, to work it out with his teachers to finish his senior year early, allowing us to do the trip in March before it got too hot. Jay, David's father, proved to be a great resource during the last couple weeks of planning. His beautiful cedar board home was situated on a small bend of the River, and had been a sort of informal headquarters for our crazy adventures for years. It had seemed like the day would never come, and now, even as I sat there in the backseat of Jay's truck, I couldn't quite believe that it was actually here.

Now, I had begun with every intention of staying awake the whole ride south, but I'm ashamed to say that after only about fifteen minutes of watching the blurred asphalt in our glow, all the adrenaline that had been pumping through me began draining away, and I soon found myself dozing off. I faded in and out, and with each new glance out the window I found that house lights were becoming fewer. Finally they vanished altogether, giving way to dense black forest silently rushing by under bright stars and a gazing moon.

I woke again. The moon was a good bit higher in the sky—I must have slept for a while that time. David was asleep against his window, snoring quietly. Jay was silent but alert, taking a sip of coffee as the pale highway unfolded out of the darkness ahead, our headlights the only source of light as far as I could see. A couple of men were talking on the radio, but he had it so low I couldn't make out the words. I recognized the bushy shape of Australian pines against the black treescape and knew we had to be a good deal farther south. I was going to ask where we were, but as I was still thinking about it my head settled into a comfortable groove in the headrest, and I was gone again.

I slept more deeply after that, waking only partially a few more times. The leather seat, which had been so cold at first, now seemed to be radiating its own soothing heat. Now and then I drowsily took in whispered words of a conversation David and Jay were having about something or other. Then, suddenly—

"Blue Cypress Lake Road!"

I jumped awake at the exclamation, forgetting for a moment where I was. My eyes were hot and stinging, and I had to wipe them hard a few times before I could see clearly. A thick, almost impenetrable fog blanketed everything, and I could barely make out the gravel road as we turned onto it. It was still dark, but it felt like dawn might be getting close—hard to tell for sure. The barely visible silhouettes of dark woods on either side drifted by like ghosts, watching as we closed in on our destination. Jay slowed to a crawl as the fog quickly worsened, and I rolled down my window, shivering at the sudden gust of cool mist. It was so quiet. A muffled chaos of pops, cracks, and crunches came from the passing gravel underneath, but the rest of the world was still, holding its breath.

After what seemed like an unbelievably long stretch of road, an old building materialized out of the fog ahead of us, along with a sign: *Middleton's Fish Camp.* We rolled to a stop just beyond it. The gravel hushed, and the sudden silence rang in our ears. We were there, only about thirty miles north of Lake Okeechobee. Somewhere—I assumed it was quite close, hidden in the mist—was Blue Cypress Lake, the womb of the St. Johns River.

"Might be worth seeing if they have any maps of the area," Jay suggested after a few moments. All three of us climbed out into the damp darkness and made our way toward the building.

Though a floodlight was blazing out from somewhere, the fog was so thick that it diffused the light into an ambiguous haze rather than giving any real visibility. Consequently, the particulars of that building remain a mystery to me; I recall it as merely a hulking old shadow with one worn, open door as we approached. We entered, and found ourselves in a fluorescent room cramped with fishing tackle, rods, cast nets, T-shirts, hats, pocket knives, and a whole host of souvenirs all bearing the name of the place. It smelled old, but a proud kind of old, the kind of smell a place gets from years of perpetual use rather than neglect.

I suddenly noticed the older woman behind the counter, who seemed to have suddenly noticed us, too. She wiped weathered hands against her plaid shirt as if she had just finished up with something and kindly nodded a greeting our way.

"Mornin' boys!" she smiled. "Where we headin' to today?" David and I looked at each other with wide grins. We were hoping someone would ask.

"We're going to the ocean!" David beamed, and we waited for a look of surprise or admiration to sweep across the woman's face. It didn't. Instead, it turned grave.

"No you're not."

The blunt response took us all by surprise, and she immediately had our full attention.

"Can't get to the ocean from here," she continued. "Ain't no outlets from this lake that you can take a boat through."

"Even a kayak?" I asked nervously.

"Oh, you've got kayaks, eh?" Even at this she seemed completely unimpressed. "So you're gonna try to take the canals?"

We nodded.

"You're gonna have quite a time getting through there this time of year. Water level's awful low right now; I doubt all those canals will even have enough water. Plus, they're putting in a new plug a few miles north of here, right across where you boys'll need to go—that'll be a gamble whether or not you'll be able to get through that construction. I see 'em bringing in more dirt every day for that thing."

I bit my lip at the report.

"Do you get people trying to do this kind of thing very often?" Jay ventured.

"We get guys every once in a while that come down here thinking they're gonna run the whole River," she scoffed, looking us up and down with a critical eye. "It's easy to talk about, but it's quite another thing to do it."

The three of us walked back toward the truck in heavy silence. The fog had lifted considerably during our time inside, and I could now see the concrete boat ramp just several yards to the east, black water as still as glass at its feet. Our path was finally clear before us. And yet, as I looked at our loaded truck with the woman's words still churning in my gut, I wavered. The solid plans and ample provisions that had had us beaming early this morning now seemed like a children's game. What were we thinking? We had no clue what we were doing! Before us lay a three hundred and ten-mile River, and here we were, two idiots with a couple of recreational kayaks, a tent, and a few bags of food. At that moment I was glad I hadn't eaten earlier, or my wrenching stomach might have heaved it up. Those dark, placid waters beyond were no longer inviting me to adventure, but like the grave seemed to gape their depths before me, eager to swallow me up somewhere out there in that haunting silence beyond.

"Well," Jay's voice suddenly broke me from my racing thoughts, "I guess it's up to you guys. That report didn't sound too promising."

No, it didn't. Who could blame us if we turned back after hearing that? I looked over at David, who was looking right back at me. The same doubts were playing in his eyes. I took in a deep breath and let it go, wisping white in the cool, damp air. We had to make a call.

Movement suddenly rippled the still face of the water—a great blue heron. He was strolling knee-deep in the black, oblivious to us, his long, thin legs reaching out one after the other, planting firmly on the hidden bottom. As I watched—I'm not sure exactly why or how—the grip of fear broke. This was a new starting point, sure, but it was the same River. We had to go. We couldn't turn back now after coming all the way down here.

"We're going," I resolved, relieved at the finality in my voice. "We can't let a little low water stop us. I'll drag Old Orange behind me if I have to!"

David laughed. "I'm with ya, buddy!"

I knew he didn't want to put any pressure on us, but I could tell that Jay was pleased with the decision, too. He climbed into the truck and backed down the boat ramp to the water's edge. The fog was now completely gone, and I was able to see for the first time that we were actually on the shore of a small inlet, sheltered by a thin strip of wooded land before us. Beyond the narrow opening that cut through it I could vaguely make out a great expanse, stretching out to the first dim grey of morning that was beginning to appear against the black sky.

NO TURNING BACK

We worked together to slide the kayaks out from the bed of the truck and load them with all the gear. They were heavier than they had ever been for any of our trips before, holding enough food and equipment for the entire journey along with three days' worth of rationed water. But even once they were fully packed they seemed weightless as they floated in the shallows, bobbing effortlessly as they awaited their pilots. David and I grabbed our paddles, icy cold from the long ride in the open air, and all three of us stood there in silence for a moment. A gentle wind brushed through the trees, but the water at our feet remained black glass.

Jay gave us both a firm handshake. "You guys take care, now," he smiled, "and Godspeed."

My heart was pounding as I settled myself into Old Orange, sending out silent ripples as the craft balanced my weight. The feeling was so familiar to me, that sensation of being suspended between the two worlds of water and air, held perfectly between so that neither had complete power over me. I was where I belonged—I was ready. I exchanged a nod with David who sat ready in New Blue, took a deep breath, and sunk one of my paddle blades into the darkness, gurgling and eddying the surface as I pulled. Our journey had begun.

We quickly gained speed, and within just moments we had made our way through the narrow pass of the inlet and got our first unobstructed view of Blue Cypress Lake in the predawn light. The breeze tugged playfully at my hat with a refreshing chill as we made our way out into the open water. Jay watched us until the trees swallowed him up from view, and then we were on our own, passing into wilderness.

David laughed as we picked up speed across the calm waters. "I can't believe we're actually doing this!"

"Neither can I!"

A dull amethyst glow slowly leaked out from the grey horizon, followed quickly by streaks of reds and oranges that stained the heavens with fire. The deep water around us changed with it, casting off its dark mantle and donning the pulsing vibrance overhead, shattering it into living diamonds of light which lapped cheerfully against my bow as I cut through them. For a few precious minutes we were awash in it all until the colors slowly retreated into pastels, and finally the pure gold of true morning began to grow as we neared the eastern shore. The sun crested the dense cypress trees in a welcomed coronation, and under the young blueing sky we could make out more details.

"I can see the opening of the canal," David called a little ways ahead of me, "just over there!"

I followed his pointing and saw it, too—a small sliver cutting through the thick swamp forest that enveloped the shoreline. The wind became more persistent as the sun rose above the trees, roughing up the lake a bit, but everything instantly hushed back to a calm as we reached the shelter of the canal. There at the opening we stopped for a moment to get some water and a small snack.

The way that lay before us was unlike anything I had ever seen before. The canal ran perfectly straight as far as I could see to the north, testifying that its flow was indeed manmade, yet the berms on either side were covered in dense, jungle-like trees and vines which gave the sense of a natural landscape. It was a surreal contrast. Add to this the gentle mist that still hung over the surface of the water here, and it was as if we had entered into some kind of dream world.

After our short break we continued on. With the absence of almost any current at all, our bows seemed for a time to be the only things disturbing the lazy waters of the canal as we made our way through the mist. Eventually, a small alligator surfaced several yards ahead, then dove again in a hurry as he spotted us.

"We should keep track of how many alligators we see," David suggested. "That was one."

"Two," I added just a few moments later, spying one slowly making its way into the pickerel weed against the west bank.

Our canal ran for nearly four and a half miles and we covered the distance in slightly more than an hour, our gator count having grown to sixteen. A large water control structure now stretched out before us, blocking our passage—the first plug.

"Whoa, seventeen!" David shouted as a huge fifteen-foot blur of scaly grey splashed into the water just ahead of us. The waves rocked our boats as we followed a shallow little channel that cut into the western shore and ended at the steep embankment to the left of the plug. An airboat ramp made of thick weathered boards ran up to the top, roughly twelve feet above the water, but beyond that our way was hidden.

"Let's take the ramp," David suggested. "I'll grab the fronts of the kayaks, you can grab the backs, and we can get them up and over in one trip."

We wasted no time putting the plan into action, eager to keep up a good pace, but had forgotten after a few hours on the water just how heavy the boats were. Merely hauling them up onto the shore was surprisingly difficult since the ground was somewhat soft. Still, it was much too early in the trip for something so small to discourage us, and we began plodding our way little by little up the old ramp, one boat in each straining, white-knuckled hand. There was space between the wooden boards and the ground underneath—I could tell by the hollow thuds that our heavy footfalls were making on them—but they would hold us.

"Break!" I called, and we quickly dropped our loads, shaking the sting out of our fingers and wiping our brows. We were only about a quarter of the way to the top. We bore up the kayaks again, fighting our way up inch by inch. My legs started burning. A drop of sweat ran down my forehead and stung my eye.

"Break!" This time it was David who called it. We were halfway. "This is a little harder than I thought!" he laughed, using the bottom of his shirt to mop his face.

"All the way to the top this time!" I encouraged. "Let's just push through and get it over with."

David gave a nervous smile and breathed deep. "Ok, let's go!"

I heaved up the heavy load again, hands burning. "Almost there," I told myself.

One step, two steps, three steps...

Another bead of sweat ran off the edge of my nose.

Four steps, five steps, six steps...

My left leg almost gave out, but I lunged forward with my right to stop a fall. I could hear David straining ahead of me.

"Almost there!" I shouted. "Push through it and let's get this done!"

Seven steps, eight steps...

Points of light danced across my vision as I watched David clear the top. My head swam but I fought against it, summoning all the strength I had left in me and lunging upward until, finally, we leveled out and dropped the boats. We sat for a few minutes, catching our breath in silence as we looked around. There was a neglected dirt road running along the top just about as far as we could see from east to west. Down the other side of the ramp, to our relief, the canal continued ahead of us.

"Ok," I encouraged, "a little walk downhill and we're done. We've still got a long way to go yet—you ready?"

David gave a nod, gave his hands one more shake, and got back into position. He shouted a three count and we began slowly plodding down the other side with our heavy load, rattling the old boards as we went. On this side there were no trees, and the berms were bare dirt. The channel made a quick zigzag ahead of us, but beyond that I couldn't make it out.

A subtle buzzing noise brought me back to my immediate surroundings. Electricity? No, it was a different kind of buzzing. I looked down and saw the culprits: a couple of lone bees circling my legs.

"Bees," I observed casually, not thinking much of it.

"What?" David called back as we continued stomping.

A few more bees appeared, moving a bit more aggressively now.

"Bees," I repeated a little louder.

"What?"

At that moment the quiet buzzing suddenly became a roar. I looked down to see a horrible black cloud of bees, hundreds strong, come swarming up through the old wooden planks underneath me.

"Bees!" I screamed.

The furious black cloud enveloped me, and the peaceful stillness was cut through with the drone of endless angry wings. The first sting on my leg sent adrenaline tingling through me in an instant, then another sting followed quickly after. I dropped the boats and took off back up the ramp as several more stings bit into my legs, then my arms. I heard David shout from somewhere behind me but I couldn't see him; I was surrounded by the chaos. I swatted blindly into the swarm, hoping that once I was a good distance away from the hive they would lose interest in me, but as I reached the dirt road at the top of the plug the stings kept coming unabated.

I simply couldn't get them all off of me. They were up under my hat, tangling themselves in my hair and piercing my scalp; they were burrowing under the sleeves and down the neck of my shirt; they were jostling into the legs of my shorts. The ones I managed to swat away were immediately replaced by more. They crawled and pelted and stung with a speed and violence that was beyond belief. That's just about when I truly panicked.

I leapt into a westward sprint down the dirt road, but the swarm kept up with me as if I were standing still and the stings kept coming. I yanked my hat off and desperately whipped it around my head in a futile attempt to sweep some away. A sting pierced my face close to my right eye—fortunately, I was wearing sunglasses. Another sent fire up the back of my neck. My heart was racing and my lungs were burning, but I kept running for my life at full speed. Two—three stings into my left arm, then two more on my right. Two on the back of my right leg. One bee latched onto my beard and stung my cheek. I kept running, flailing like a madman.

Just when I felt my legs would give out from under me, the droning died down, and as quickly as the swarm had appeared it fell away. I crumpled to the ground, heaving for breath and shaking from the combination of fear and exhaustion. I was nearly a quarter mile from the boats, but David was about a hundred yards farther, swatting violently with his hat in hand.

It wasn't quite over yet; a few devotees remained, hoping to get the last few stings. One darted into my hair, but with my rushing adrenaline I reacted instantly and squashed it. One of its comrades flew straight into my face—I swatted that one off, too, but didn't notice the one that grabbed onto my neck and paid for it with yet another painful sting. I slapped it off, still gasping for breath. I looked over at David, who met my gaze with wide eyes.

"What are we gonna do!" he had barely shouted the words before dodging another attack.

I didn't answer—I didn't know! Another latched onto my right arm and I slapped it away. What *were* we going to do? But then, all at once, I suddenly came to my senses. There was no way, absolutely no way we were going to be stopped by a bunch of maniac insects! The fear that had gripped me melted away into a focused fury.

I straightened up as another bee landed on me. I took a second to concentrate and aim this time, no longer fearing a sting, and squashed it against my leg. Another came whizzing around my head. I froze, followed its darting movements, then delivered a direct hit with my hat, sending it stunned to the ground. I crushed it under my right sandal—I had lost the left one at some point in my sprint—and turned to face the last two whirling above me.

"Sting me!" I shouted at them. "Do it! I dare you to sting me again!" One of them took a dive toward me, but I planted that one into the ground as well. "Come on!" I pointed to the other one. "Bring it! Come on!" I didn't care at that point that I was yelling at a bee. It hesitated a moment, hovering almost motionless in the sky, then fell back toward the boat ramp and disappeared into the distance.

I ran over to where David was still contending with a few more. I followed one for a moment and knocked it out of the sky. It crunched under my sandal. David paused to do the same and got another one.

Another crunch. The last one dove down from above, but was also sent to the ground. We stood in triumph over our fallen foe flailing in the dust, and with a shout of rage David knelt down and flattened it into the ground with his fist. He got back up slowly, flicking a small piece of gravel from his bloody knuckles, and we stood gasping together in the blessed stillness.

We didn't say a word for some time. As my heartbeat slowly returned to its normal rhythm I felt the adrenaline drain out of my limbs, giving way to a painful, pulsing heat radiating from the stingers all over me. I winced as I yanked a couple out from my cheek and behind my ear, then looked over at David. David looked at me. We stared at each other for a moment, then slowly smiled, then burst out laughing.

"Bees!" David imitated my scream from earlier, tears beginning to roll down his face. "Man, I never saw you run so fast!"

"Well you ended up farther than I did!" I countered, wiping a few tears of my own. "That was one of the craziest things I've ever seen!"

"It looked just like the swarms in Saturday morning cartoons! Always thought they were exaggerating it, but now I know better!"

We eventually got ourselves back under control and returned to the serious situation at hand with somewhat lighter hearts.

"Now, how in the world are we gonna get those boats?" David wondered as we began walking slowly back toward the ramp.

"Let's get close enough to see what the area looks like before we start thinking," I suggested. "Maybe they're already back in the hive and we can just sneak around it."

But the bees were not back in their hive. As we came closer, we could make out the swarming mass darting about the sterns of the kayaks, looking like they had no intention of settling down any time soon. We froze as we heard buzzing again, and a lone bee whacked straight into my face. Without a word I swatted it to the ground and crunched it. No more came.

"Must have been a scout," I chuckled, and pulled a few more stingers out of my arm as we assessed the situation. "Ok, what about this? We head down to the water's edge right here where we are and approach the boat ramp from the bottom. The hive is closer to the top and most of the bees are up there. If we're really slow and quiet we might be able to grab the bows of the kayaks, yank them down the rest of the way to the water, then run off before the bees can attack. Once they settle back down, we approach the ramp from the bottom again, jump in and paddle like crazy till we're out of here."

David took a moment to think it through. "What if there are bees in the kayaks?"

"We'll just have to deal with one thing at a time, I guess."

We carefully made our way down the grassy embankment to the water's edge, still about forty yards west of the ramp. We closed in slowly, watching the swarm for any movements our way. After what seemed like an hour of suspense we finally reached the bows of the boats without incident.

"Okay," I whispered, "my kayak is closest, so you'd better get ahead of me so we can grab them at the same time. You ready?"

David took a deep breath. "Let's do it. One...two...three!"

I gave David a split-second head start and then dashed after him onto the wooden planks. We were so close to the swarm that I could hear the angry droning. I reached Old Orange, firmly grabbed the toggle hanging from the bow and gave it a powerful heave, sending her clattering down to the water. I steadied her to keep her from sliding out into the canal and then sprinted back westward, imagining the bees just behind me. As I rejoined with David, however, I realized that they hadn't even taken notice of us.

"Did you have any chase you?" I asked.

David shook his head. "Looks like we're in the clear. Let's go back the same way again and get out of here."

We repeated the route, going down through the soggy grass and approaching from the water's edge where the boats were waiting undisturbed. We stepped out cautiously onto the wooden planks once more, quickly inspecting the insides.

"I don't see any bees in mine," David reported.

"I'm good, too. Let's go!"

We jumped in and pushed off in a flash, listening carefully as the buzzing of the swarm died away for the last time. We were finally free, back on the water again!

"Wow," David heaved a sigh of relief as we rounded the bend, "I definitely didn't plan for that!"

"From now on," I laughed, "we're carrying these things on the grass!"

I kept finding new stingers to pry out all over me, but fortunately the sting of the venom was already subsiding. If I had been allergic to it, I would have surely died right there on that dusty road in the middle of nowhere. I took a deep breath, grateful to have been spared, and whispered a prayer of thanks as we set our gaze before us.

The canal held its northwest heading for only a bit before shifting directly northward again. Trees returned on the steep banks, and for several blessed miles we had smooth traveling until we began to notice distant, chaotic noises disrupting the quiet.

"What do you suppose...?" David's voice trailed off as he strained to identify the sound.

After a bit farther, our canal seemed to end up ahead at an overgrown swampy bank.

"Maybe it turns a little to the east and then swings back around," I suggested hopefully, but I had a bad feeling in the pit of my stomach.

We drew even closer and finally the noise became clear: construction equipment! It eventually grew so loud that it drowned out everything else. My heart leaped as I saw that the canal did indeed turn to the east, but as we cleared the bend we were met with a definite dead end at the base of a freshly built dirt embankment, rising nearly eight feet above the water. A dump truck was pulling up to the edge and adding a huge mound to the already enormous construction, sending boulder-sized chunks of earth rolling down its face and crashing into the water before us. The ripples gently bobbed the boats as we slowed to a stop and watched.

With its bed now empty, the dump truck headed back along the embankment, and a bulldozer chugged up to grade out the newly dropped pile. David waved at the operator a couple of times before he finally spotted us and stopped the machine. My ears rang in the sudden silence as he opened the cab and climbed out.

"Hey," David called up to him, "is there any way we could cross over this thing real quick?"

The man shook his head. "Sorry boys, can't let you come up here while all these trucks are runnin' back and forth. But you can walk across that," he pointed to the swampy dead end of the canal. "It doesn't look like it from where you're at, but it'll hold ya." With that, he climbed into the bulldozer and went back to work.

It didn't seem like we had much of a choice. I ran Old Orange into the soggy bank, threw my boots on, and stepped out cautiously. I sank an inch or two into the mud, but that was all—the bulldozer guy had been right. David joined me.

"Let's walk a little to the far side of this before we start hauling the boats," I suggested. "Pulling them all the way through this stuff is going to be time consuming enough as it is; we can at least make sure we know where we need to take them."

The two of us sloshed carefully through the muck, keeping our guard up for alligators or cottonmouths hidden in the high grass. We made our way around a small clump of dead trees and finally caught sight of where the water appeared again, nearly three hundred yards north of where we were standing.

I sighed. "It's gonna take us an hour to get the boats through here...this isn't looking good at all."

David agreed with the estimate. "We'll have to take them one at a time; it's too narrow to take them both at once. I guess we'd better get on with it."

We made the short trek back with heavy hearts, and were preparing to grab Old Orange when the man in the bulldozer shouted back over at us.

"Boys! Hey boys! The guys are going on their lunch break, so you can go ahead and bring your boats up here!"

I couldn't hold back a wide grin as I breathed a sigh of relief. "Thanks so much!" I hollered back. "You just saved us a lot of work!"

The man slid his way down to the water's edge to meet us, and even helped us pull the boats up onto the road before he left to take his own break.

"Thanks again!" we shouted after him as he set off down the dirt path.

We waddled the boats across the top of the embankment, slowly but surely making our way around the swampy area that had blocked our way and arriving at the water on the other side. It took a bit of time to safely lower them back down the almost vertical crumbling slope, but we finally managed it without incident. Between the portages and the bees we had lost some time, but now at least we were back on course! That next hour we encountered no more obstacles until another plug appeared up ahead.

"This should be the last of them," I told David as we once more pulled onto shore.

There was no wooden airboat jump here, just a wide sandy trail that ran gently up to the top of the plug. I grabbed the bow of Old Orange, dragged her up to the peak, and found myself looking down on clear, shallow water rippled with white sandbars.

"Looks like we're going to be walking for a little while," I shouted back to David, who was still at the bottom on the south side.

His shoulders slumped. "Are you serious? We can't get a break today!"

We rested for a few minutes on top of the plug, grabbing some water and food. I munched on peanut butter crackers as I sat on the stern of Old Orange.

"You know, this day has been pretty rough so far, but in all honesty it could have been a lot worse."

"Yeah," David chuckled, "there could have been bees here, too!"

"We could have been caught in a bad storm, or in extreme heat, but it's a gorgeous day." I hesitated for a moment. "How's your shoulder? Any issues?"

David had a problem with the rotator cuff in his right shoulder that would come and go. It didn't bother him too much when paddling a canoe, but the windmill-like motion of kayaking had sometimes aggravated it in the past. I was relieved to see him smile and shake his head.

"Feels fine so far," he said, giving his arm a couple of rotations as proof.

"Good. Let me know if you need to take it easy or anything, okay?"

"Sure will."

As I had predicted, we had to walk the boats through the shallow water for several hundred yards. I was concerned that the rest of the canal might go on like that, but soon enough the water deepened and we were able to start paddling again. While the banks of the canals near Blue Cypress Lake had been overgrown and blended into the landscape, the stretch we now traveled through was dry and dead. Most of the trees and grasses were brown and rotting on the banks, and at the top of the eastern embankment there was only a thin line of scraggly brush between us and an old dirt road running along the top. It was not a very inviting place, and I was anxious to finally get to the natural River.

After the last plug, the next hour of our trip was uneventful. We kept paddling north down the perfectly straight canal until we started to wonder if it had an end at all. Had we missed the turnoff? How much farther should we go before we turned around to try and find it? But just as we began to seriously consider going back, an opening appeared in the west bank, and as we took it the River abandoned its rigid, man-made confines and took on a meandering course in a northwesterly direction. At first the banks were still five or six feet high like they had been in the canal, but these banks seemed to be carved out by the River itself, not by man. Neat, barren berms became dark, jagged bluffs, crowned with clumps of waving grasses that gently whispered over our heads as we passed by.

I tensed as I felt the soft, grainy scratching of the river bottom rub the underside of the boat—it was getting shallower. As we rounded another bend I felt it again. The next bend I almost got stuck. The woman at Middleton's had said that the water level was just about at an all-time low...what if we ran out of water altogether? What if we turned a bend and there was nothing as far as we could see but miles of black muck where water once ran? I bit my lip at the prospect, but quickly forced the thought out of my mind; it wouldn't do any good to worry about it now. If we ran out of water, we would figure out what to do.

One encouragement was the first evidence of a fairly steady current running with us, and as a result the meander of the River became more pronounced. The insides of each bend now tapered slowly down into the water, making half of the channel too shallow to use, and we were forced to travel single file on the remaining eight feet or so of the outsides where the water was deepest. Though we often brushed bottom, we always seemed to have just enough depth to squeeze the boats through.

We went so long with our heads down watching the water that I was surprised to suddenly notice the air filled with wisps of snowy white. They were like a mix between dandelion seeds and cotton, floating silently on the gentle breeze.

"Now this is something you don't see every day!" David smiled as he blew at a few clumps by his face.

They were from the coastal plain willows, I realized, which were now dominating both shores. They were covered with the fluff, which was really countless millions of their seeds. The wind was shaking their shaggy crowns of slender leaves, making their light undersides flash like fireworks as they caught the sun, and from those rustling boughs the seeds were pouring out into the air in thick clouds and covering everything like snow. We paddled through this surreal scene for nearly an hour before it finally began to clear.

All the while, we held a pretty steady northwesterly course until our meandering path emptied into another northward-running canal. Its west bank was thick with cypresses, palms, and red maples, and we stuck close under their shade as we adjusted to our new heading. Bits of sunlight and shadow danced wildly under the canopy as the breeze moved them, and the awkward crashing of the palm fronds in particular sounded like waves on a seashore above our heads. I smiled, closing my eyes for a moment and taking in the refreshing coolness rippling through my shirt and tugging playfully at the brim of my hat.

"It's been a tough day," David commented beside me, "but I'm still glad we're out here, man."

"Agreed."

That delightful little wooded bank spanned only the length of the canal, about a half mile. As the River finally broke free from the last of its man-made paths the trees once again fell away, and we were paddling through a vast marshland. It was then that the alligators began to appear en masse. Our count soared to over two hundred within the hour, and they kept coming. There were so many alligators that we were spotting ten or twenty of them at once! They would slide down from the low, muddy banks and lazily disappear into the dark water as we passed by.

Despite their intimidating appearance and sometimes enormous size, the reality is that alligators very rarely attack humans, especially in boats. I had traveled hundreds of miles on the River and could count on one hand the number of times when I had been in a dangerous situation with an alligator—those are tales for another time, perhaps. Nevertheless, I would be lying if I told you I wasn't even a little nervous. I didn't fear an intentional attack, but was concerned that with so many of them in the water with us the potential for an accident was steadily increasing. There simply wasn't that much space in the narrow channel. If we spooked one underneath us, even a small gator could cause serious damage to the boats. Once we were actually in the water with such a crowd, things could go south pretty quickly. Needless to say, we stuck pretty close together for this section.

We passed through our second lake of the day, Lake Hell 'n Blazes. Despite the tough name, we had no problem conquering its short mile-long breadth and finding the River again on the northern shore. Within another half hour we reached the even smaller Little Sawgrass Lake, followed immediately by Sawgrass Lake, which was not even a mile and a half long. We crossed them both easily, with only a little bit of chop on Sawgrass Lake from the fairly mild breeze.

It was late afternoon when we spotted a sign suspended high on a pole above the sighing reeds: *Holly's Marina*. A bridge appeared, and soon after that a cluster of small buildings to our left. As I ran Old Orange onto the grassy shore, I suddenly realized how tired I was. I crawled out and pulled her securely onto land, David doing the same with New Blue beside me.

"I didn't see this place on the maps," I squinted up at the sign again, "but maybe the people here'll let us stay the night."

"No harm in asking," David shrugged.

We carefully dusted ourselves off, made sure our hats were on straight, and started over to the small outcropping of civilization. Closest to us was an old wood frame building with a low tin roof and a large screened-in porch jutting out at the front. Just a little ways beyond it were a couple of worn aluminum storage sheds, a double-wide trailer, and a large wooden pavilion cluttered with yard equipment. We went for the first building.

As we opened the flimsy screen door and went into the porch area, we saw that the inside door was already fully open. We entered a large open room with an aged wood plank floor and a few tables and chairs positioned randomly. A small L-shaped bar was to our immediate right, upon which was a jar full of dried gator feet on key chains, each individually priced according to size. Along the walls were pinned maps, charts, a couple of newspaper clippings, and a host of both new and yellowed photographs. Sitting in a chair at the far end of the building was a middle-aged man in a fishing shirt, shorts, and worn boat shoes who was staring at us. He had a bushy mustache and a head of thin, peppered hair that was wisping in the breeze of the small fan running in the corner. He nodded our way and smiled as we came closer.

"Hey there, boys."

I tipped my hat to him and walked up to shake his hand. "Good afternoon, sir. I'm Daniel."

David repeated the gesture.

"Carl," the man introduced himself, then looked past us to where a tall bearded man with long brown hair had come out from a room behind the bar. "And that there's Danny," Carl told us, then informed Danny, "This is Daniel and David."

Danny seemed to be in no hurry with whatever he had been doing, because he left his task and came over. From our filthy, sweaty clothes, I think he suspected there might be a good story here.

"So where'd ya'll put in at?" he asked with genuine interest.

"Blue Cypress Lake, early this morning," David replied.

"Where you stoppin' at?"

"Well, hopefully the ocean; we're trying to travel the whole St. Johns River in nine days."

Carl whistled and shook his head. "You boys still got a long way to go then, huh?"

"We were wondering if you would mind us pitching a tent out by the bank over there for the night," I ventured, pointing out one of the windows to where the kayaks sat. "We'll be running out of daylight soon and you've got some nice high ground here."

"Sure," Carl replied without the slightest hesitation, "I don't mind one bit. You boys are welcome to set your tent wherever you want, but you may want to sleep under the bridge over there; they're saying there's a chance of rain tonight." I turned around and looked out through the open north-facing door. The property of the marina butted right up against the bridge only about seventy yards away.

"Is there dry ground under there?"

"Sure is," Danny replied. "Come on out a minute and I'll show ya." I followed him outside and across the empty dirt parking area. From there the bank under the bridge was clearly visible, and I could even see a worn path through the high grass leading down from where we were standing. "It's sorta muddy more toward the north side," Danny pointed, "but on this side you shouldn't have any problem finding a dry spot right underneath. If that doesn't suit ya, like Carl said, ya'll are welcome to set up wherever you want; you just might get a little wet, that's all."

As we came back inside, Danny grabbed a few supplies from the room behind the bar and got ready to head out again. "If you boys need anything at all during the night," he said as he pushed the screen door open with his foot, "I live in that double-wide just over there. Don't hesitate to knock, okay?"

"Thanks," I nodded to him, "we really appreciate it."

"We appreciate you too, sir," David tipped his hat to Carl, who had not moved from his seat.

"Ah," Carl waved it off with a grin, "think nothin' of it, boys. Glad to help."

We paddled quickly to the bridge and pulled up directly underneath it onto soft white sand. The ground there was certainly firm, but I noticed right away that there was no way we would find a root-free spot big enough for the footprint of the tent; we would just have to position ourselves around them. We had the tent set up in a matter of minutes, tossed the sleeping bags inside, then turned our minds to dinner. My meal that night consisted of a pack of tuna, a trail mix bar, some peanuts, whole wheat crackers, and a fruit cup to finish it all off—can't remember if it was the mixed fruit or the pineapple. One thing I can tell you, though, is that that short rest and hearty dinner seemed to drop all the hard work of the day right off my shoulders.

David reclined back with his elbows in the sand, watching as the clouds began to glint with the colors of the sunset at our backs. He popped a peanut butter cracker into his mouth whole, gave it a couple crunches and breathed in deep. "Has it really only been one day?" he managed to mumble as he chewed. "Seems like it's already been a week!"

"I know! This was a long day." I casually rubbed my arm, but winced as I caught a stinger I had missed. "How many times did you get stung by those bees?"

"I didn't!" David laughed, watching me yank the stinger out and toss it into the sand. "I had a few of them chase me, but you were the one right over the hive; they all wanted you, I guess!"

"I'd be just fine if we never find any more of those out here."

"I'm not gonna lie, I was terrified, man!" David said it with a smile, but then added a little more soberly, "That could have been really bad back there."

The sky was gold now, and for a few moments the whole world seemed ageless in its glow. I shivered as a cooler breeze began whispering up from the water, heralding the twilight that was soon to come.

"Carl said they'd keep the bathrooms open for us all night," David reported as he chewed up his last cracker and sealed his food bag. "Apparently they've even got showers in there!"

"Are you telling me you're gonna take a shower the first day of the trip?"

"Well, why not? Between the dust, the dirt, and the mud, we certainly got dirty enough for it!"

I sealed up my bag, too. "You might as well get used to it, pal! We've got another eight days of this at best; showering now is only prolonging the inevitable."

"Don't care." He got up and fished around in the back of New Blue until he had found a fresh pair of clothes.

"Wow, new clothes too, eh?" I smirked. "Well, won't you just be the Lily of the River!"

"Ya, ya, ya," David ignored me as he began his short trek back to the marina. "If things get bad later, I'll throw on this dirty pair again if I have to."

I unzipped the door of the tent and crawled in, careful to clear my feet of sand before swinging them in after me. I was always amazed at how much bigger it was than it appeared to be on the outside. Don't get me wrong, it was no mansion! Still, it was comfortable, just enough room for two sleeping bags and a bit of gear. My sleeping bag was rolled out and ready in a matter of seconds, then I pulled out my worn leather journal. As I did, an envelope fell out from between the pages. My fiance, Nicole, had given it to me only the night before, putting on the bravest face she could in a vain attempt to hide her worry. Inside were letters from her for every day of the trip; I had forgotten all about them until that moment! The light was fading from gold to grey against the fabric walls, but there was still enough light left to find the first one. I broke the seal and opened it.

I know you are so excited about the big trip, and I am, too. You're going to do amazing. I know that you will be strong and have the endurance and faith to finish. As you embark on this life-changing experience, I hope you know that I will be praying for you. I love you so much! Be safe!

I smiled, wedged the envelope securely into the leather sleeve, then took a few minutes to quickly jot down the events of the day. I squinted harder and harder, moving my face closer and closer as the last of the pale light slowly disappeared. I could barely see my last few words as I finally finished my entry and returned the journal to its home.

The single floodlight at the marina kicked on and hummed low, washing my side of the tent in a soft orange glow, and only a few minutes later David's giant walking shadow projected against it. It shrunk with each step he took down the path to the water's edge until I could hear his feet kicking up the sand. The opening unzipped and he stumbled in, filling the air with the crisp smell of soap.

"How you feeling, princess?" I chuckled as he unrolled his sleeping bag next to mine.

"Laugh it up," he replied, unashamed, "I'm going to be the one sleeping good tonight."

"Oh, I think after that thirty miles of paddling today I'll sleep just fine. Is your shoulder sore at all?"

David pulled his arm back a couple of times. "Not really, my back's just pretty tight. You?"

"About the same."

"I feel pretty good about today," David reflected as he crawled into his sleeping bag. "I mean, we definitely had some obstacles, but we still made good time."

"I'm more concerned about tomorrow; it'll be the longest day of the whole trip."

"How far?"

"We've got to do thirty-seven miles to get to the next stopping point. We'll have to keep up a brisk pace just about all day. Think you're up to it?"

"We'll make it," David replied confidently.

My eyelids were getting heavy as I balled up my shirt for a pillow. The crickets were out now, their songs pulsing from the far bank of the River. The tent rippled drowsily in the cool night breeze, but other than that the world was still. I gasped as I sunk into my sleeping bag, the fabric catching yet another stinger in my leg that I had missed—I yanked it out the rest of the way and tossed it into the dark. Settling in, I felt myself drifting off in a hurry, riding the cricket's lullaby to a deep sleep.

THE SOUTHERN LAKES

I jumped awake as a semi-truck roared over the bridge above us. I groped frantically in the darkness, forgetting for a moment where I was, but quickly it all came back to me—day two. It was nearly half past six. The alarm was due to go off in a few minutes anyway, so I went ahead and rolled up my sleeping bag. David was still sound asleep.

I hoisted my food bag between my legs and opened it up, clicked on my small flashlight, and fished around until I found my store of granola. I was crunching down a handful when the alarm went off, and I waited for David to jump, roll over, move an arm, any sign of life. Nothing. I leaned over and turned it off.

"David, let's go man, it's time to get ready."

At the sound of my voice he was instantly awake. He sat up and rubbed his eyes. "What time is it?"

"About half past. We've got an hour or so before sunrise so we've gotta get moving."

David quickly grabbed breakfast and packed his sleeping bag. We loaded all our gear back into the boats and then broke down the tent. Everything was stowed and ready by 7:00.

David nodded to the water jug in his boat that was three-quarters empty. "I've got two more of those, but since we're at a marina we might as well see if we can fill them back up."

"Yeah, I drank a whole jug yesterday. I don't know what kind of water they've got coming out of their spigots, but I guess it'll be better than nothing in an emergency."

We each grabbed our depleted jugs and made one last walk over to Holly's Marina. To our surprise the lights were on and a man was already there, though as we got closer I realized it wasn't Carl or Danny.

"Howdy," he nodded as we walked in. "You the boys that were sleepin' under the bridge last night?"

"That's us," David said. "We were wondering if we could fill up our water jugs somewhere. Do you guys have a hose or something we could use?"

The man made a face of disgust. "Ah! Ya'll are travelin' the whole River, ain't ya?"

We nodded.

"Well then, you ain't drinkin' from no hose if I've got anything to say about it. Come on over here in the back." Curious, we followed him back behind the bar and into a small storage room. He flicked on the light and scooted out a five-gallon water jug with a pump nozzle on top. "This here is the well water I bring in from home," he explained; "best water you've ever tasted in your life."

"Our water jugs are pretty big," I warned, showing him, "we wouldn't want you to use all that on us."

"Nah, there's plenty," he insisted. "You boys'll need it."

David chuckled nervously as the man took our jugs. "What's that supposed to mean? Is there anything we need to look out for?"

"Nothin' in particular," the man said as he began to pump the water, "just the weir at the north end of Lake Washington."

I knew about the weir, of course, but had never actually seen it before. "Think we should be able to get our kayaks over easily enough?" I asked cautiously.

"Oh, you shouldn't have any problems getting over, but I hear the water's pretty shallow right now once you get past it. You boys may be doing some walkin' today."

"It's *that* dry?" David asked, surprised. I was as well.

"Now, mind you, I haven't been down there in a few months," the man shrugged, "I'm only telling you what I've heard from air boaters that have passed by here. They've been sayin' that between Lake Washington and Lake Winder it's pretty hairy right now. But who knows? Them boats of yours are so small that maybe you'll get through after all. Hard to say."

"What about after Lake Winder?" I probed, searching for some hope that I could hold on to for the day. "After that we shouldn't have any problems?"

The man passed my jug back to me full and began filling David's. "No, you oughta have plenty of water once you get past Winder." Then he chuckled, "After that your problem might be too much water, what with Lake Poinsett and all. That's one big lake! I hope you boys have experience with stuff like that."

David smiled. "We've got a bit of experience under our belts. It's the *no* water part right after the weir that concerns me the most. It's awful hard to kayak when you've got nothing to kayak in!"

"Well, I wish you boys safe travels," he said, handing back a full jug to David.

After thanking the man, we quickly headed back to the boats in the grey of the approaching dawn.

"Sunrise is at 7:30," I observed, "but it starts getting light around 7:00. We should probably get up a little earlier from now on and use this predawn light for traveling."

"Yeah, any distance we can knock out before the sun comes up is okay by me!"

By 7:15 we were out on the water, and Holly's Marina quickly fell out of sight as we began our second day. Matted masses of giant reed towered along both banks, motionless against the grey sky. Everything was quiet; it seemed as if the world had not quite woken up yet.

The morning came uneventfully, dabbing the cloudless horizon with the dull colors of a washed-out Polaroid before daylight quickly took its place. We were both a little stiff from the day before, but traveled easily through the glassy water. By the time we reached the southern shore of Lake Washington we were all warmed up, arriving within merely half an hour after leaving camp, faster than either of us had predicted. Though I knew the far shore lay some four miles to the north, I couldn't see more than two hundred yards in front of us because of a dense fog that sat on the lake's surface, diffusing the fresh rays of sunlight into an ambient glow.

"I'll keep us heading north through this," David called over, glancing down at his open compass. "This is some thick stuff, isn't it?"

"Sure is. I can't see anything."

We entered the calm waters of Lake Washington, and everything was quickly swallowed up in white. The fog did not last long, though. It thinned as the sun rose higher above the horizon, and by the time we had traveled about half the length of the lake it had completely vanished, leaving us with a clear view all around us. I could see the far shore now as a thick strip of green in the distance, but the view of that northern sky was not so comforting; threatening black clouds were moving steadily toward us. I couldn't quite place it, but there was something odd about the way the sunlight and shadow played on them that made me nervous.

"What do you make of that," I nodded their way.

David was already squinting into the distance as he paddled next to me. "Hard to say...there's something weird about it. We might be getting some rain."

"You got your rain poncho handy?"

"It's in a spot where I can grab it if I need it."

We continued paddling straight for the strange clouds, undeterred, and they seemed to move faster as they closed in. I gradually realized why the light fell so strangely on them. The clouds were not one great mass at all, but rather a series of vast, dark bands at least half a mile thick and spanning to the horizon, each separated from one another. The first of the bands advanced out over the lake, and the northern shoreline was suddenly consumed by a dark grey mist that appeared to be moving along with its counterpart in the sky.

"I've never seen anything like that before," I heard David mutter.

It was closing in rapidly. I couldn't see a thing through that mist. It looked more like smoke, swirling and fuming as if the surface of the lake was burning. The sparkling water around us faded as the first wisps of black in the sky choked out the morning light. In the sickly grey, that plume of black murk coming at us took on a greater terror, seeming to be swallowing up everything in its path. There was nowhere to go—it was upon us.

"Here we go!" I shouted, picking up speed to meet it head on.

A sudden powerful gust of icy wind burst at me, taking my breath away, and as the blackness enveloped me I lost nearly all visibility. The wind blew hard and cold, and ragged waves began slapping the bow as I forced my way forward.

"What is this!" David's dark silhouette called over, his voice nearly snatched away in the gale.

I could feel the blackness swirling around my face and arms, seeping into my clothes and my hat as I kept paddling. It was surreal, like one of those dreams where you are trying to get somewhere but can't make any progress. I could see Old Orange and the trembling wind-torn water immediately around me, but beyond that there was absolutely nothing, not even the sky. The mist had taken everything. Another powerful gust flared up the brim of my hat, trying to take it from me, but it held tight.

"David, you still there?"

"Yeah...where are you?"

"Over here!"

"Where's that?"

"Don't worry about it, just keep paddling!"

I began to shiver in my T-shirt and bathing suit, not having planned for such an encounter, but I grit my teeth and paddled harder against the wind as it whipped in my ears. I was becoming disoriented—were we even going north anymore? But then something caught my eye.

"Hey!" I shouted, "I think I see a little bit of light up ahead!"

Even as the words were leaving my mouth the darkness vanished, the wind hushed, the sun came out, and just like that I was suddenly back in the world of light. David reappeared only ten yards to the east, and we exchanged faces of bewilderment.

The grey mist continued moving south in a now silent fury under the shadow of its cloud band, and the next one was closing in only a few hundred yards north of us. We were right in the middle, in the calm between two monstrous walls of darkness. The sight was impossible to describe. It was one of the strangest things I had ever seen, bringing to mind thoughts of Moses parting the Red Sea. For a few moments all we could do was stare motionless.

"Let's keep moving," I finally called to David. "We've got less than two miles until we reach the other side."

The second band blotted out the sun as we started up again. The winds returned, the temperature dropped, and the mist covered us, though it was not quite as dark as the first. We fought our way against the wind for several long minutes until, just like the last time, it all vanished in an instant and the sun reappeared. I took note that the temperature had now dropped several degrees from what it had been; it seemed that every pass of those clouds was bringing in cooler air.

We were now aiming straight for the northwest corner of the lake where I knew the River would reappear. The third band hit several minutes later, but this time as we passed out of the mist the gusting winds continued even after the sun had returned. One final band was making its way toward us, and beyond that the big sky was threateningly dark. I could just barely make out dense columns of rain falling far off in the distance.

The last band and accompanying mist passed through, and quickly after it an endless sea of thick grey clouds quenched the sun, submerging the whole landscape in stormy shadows. But we barely took notice of any of this now; the opening of the River had finally come into view, and we were dead set on getting out of that lake and having a rest. We angled our boats more westward now, winding our way through mazes of golden reeds growing up out of the shallowing water. The northern and western shores of Lake Washington began to quickly converge, forming a westward-facing funnel that finally led us back to the St. Johns.

Then something caught my eye a couple hundred yards ahead...or rather an absence of something. From where we were it looked as if the River just suddenly stopped, like someone had taken a giant knife and cut it off in a perfectly straight line. The dark water flowed normally until that point, and then it simply disappeared. An airboat jump dropped out of sight beyond the impossible terminus on the south, and a narrow walkway did the same on the north side. I kept staring at the sight, trying to make sense of what my eyes were seeing. Suddenly it clicked: we had reached the Lake Washington Weir.

Several boats were tied up by the airboat jump, and a group of men were fishing off of it. Only one boat bobbed gently on the north side, and I could make out one man and a dog standing near the peak of the walkway. We headed for the less populated side, gradually getting a better and better view over the unnatural horizon of water ahead of us. The River reemerged about ten feet below, but its size was pitifully diminished. Above the weir, the breadth of the channel was about sixty yards, but below it was fifteen feet at best, more like a small creek. The shallow waters were pockmarked by sandbars and clumps of duckweed.

We tied off at the small dock, and had barely stepped out before the shaggy old mutt we had seen hurried over to inspect us. The tips of his nails clattered on the aluminum panels as he trotted down the walkway and eyed us curiously. He came in close, took one good whiff of me, and drew back a bit.

"Get back up here!" his owner, a man in his fifties, hollered at him from the top of the walkway. The dog obediently returned to his side. He looked down at us. "Sorry 'bout that, boys!"

"Oh, don't worry about it," I replied, "we don't mind dogs at all."

We hauled our food bags up onto the dock and dug around to make a meal. I pulled out an energy bar, a fruit cup, peanuts, almonds, and some dried pineapple, then shoved them all into my pockets and joined the man at the top. He was silently looking out over the vast stretch of marshland to the west, standing precisely over the top of the weir which was about six or seven feet below him. Only from there could I see the giant concrete wall that divided the two landscapes, allowing only a small flow of the River's power through outlets at the bottom on either side. A thin, almost silent waterfall spilled over the top and down its slimy grey surface.

The man's long silver hair and unkempt white beard were shuddering in the breeze. The lines on his face were more pronounced than they probably would have been without the deep shadows cast by the cloudy sky, but though he was worn he showed no signs of frailty. I shook his hand.

"Morning!" he smiled as David came up behind me, half of a granola bar already gone in his hand. "Where'd you boys put in at?"

"We put in at Blue Cypress Lake," I replied, unwrapping my energy bar and taking a bite. "We're on our second day."

"Do you know that part of the River well?" David nodded to the meager ribbon of water winding off into the west.

"I did," the man said, "until they put this thing in here. It changed everything. The water dried up, all the trees on the banks died, and all the fish left. That isn't really even the River anymore, just a skeleton of what it used to be, especially right now with water levels so low. My friends and I used to come out here years ago, and this whole area was loaded with fish. The banks were all lush and green, it was gorgeous! There was sort of a half dam that had been here for decades, less than a mile that way," he pointed west. "It held back the water a little, but it didn't span the whole way across. It was open in the middle so that the River could always flow...but not anymore."

The two of us ate in solemn silence as the man continued gazing into the west, recalling those days that were now forever confined to memories, days irrevocably lost under the concrete behemoth which stood just beneath our feet. A great blue heron called out mournfully somewhere to the north, hidden in the marshes. It was a dismal sight. It would have been depressing enough under blue skies, but under the stormy grey the landscape beyond looked truly grim, almost repulsive. Nearly ten minutes had passed before we realized that, regardless of the conditions ahead, we had to get going.

David and I rattled back down the walkway to the kayaks and hauled them up. It was so narrow that we had to go single file, but the portage was not difficult. Soon enough we were in the shallow waters below with the giant wall looming over us. We waved goodbye to the man and his dog as we set out once more, but our trip only lasted a minute or two.

Without the sun, the water was quite dark and difficult to see through, so I quickly stuck Old Orange into a hidden sandbar. David jerked to a halt several yards to the left of me. I tried to scoot over the obstruction, but had no success. Standing up carefully to get a higher view, I could just make out a stretch of rippling sand that ran for some distance over the whole width of the River.

"It's no good," I called over to David, "we'll have to walk them."

There was no time for disappointment; nothing we could do or say would change our course. There was only one way to Lake Winder, and we would have to take it one way or another. David and I kicked off our sandals in unison and stepped out, the swift-moving water barely even reaching our ankles. We each dug out a length of rope from our gear, fastened them around the toggles of the bows, and without hesitation continued on foot, splashing through the shallows with Old Orange and New Blue in tow. As we turned the bend, the last bit of the weir disappeared behind the high grasses, and it was just us again.

After several minutes the River deepened, and we happily climbed back into the boats, paddling hard to make up for lost time. Despite the low water, the current was noticeably faster here than it had been for our entire trip so far, and the grassy banks seemed to fly by as we raced single file down the narrow stretch. As we turned a bend we saw two sun-bleached walls jutting out into the current, one from each bank. They were not smooth and uniform, but seemed to have been constructed with piles of concrete sacks. Many places were cracked and crumbled, and patches of flowering grasses were sprouting from the imperfections. It must have been the old half dam the man had been telling us about.

The swift current quickly funneled us through the opening between the two walls, and they were soon out of sight as we turned another bend. I grinned as I watched the shore hurry along. At these marvelous speeds, I dared to think that today might not end up being as bad as we'd feared...but that hope only lasted for about ten seconds.

As we cleared the next bend, both banks suddenly dropped down to water level, mixing with the River to form stagnant black muck on either side. The water stilled, and only a moment later Old Orange jerked to a halt, her bow jammed into the shallow bottom only a couple inches beneath the surface. I didn't allow myself to hesitate—it wouldn't get any deeper by waiting. David and I both jumped out, took up the ropes at our bows, and began our second walk of the day, upsetting a large flock of ibis which scolded us with gruff squawks.

Though the banks looked pretty disgusting, the middle of the River was firm under our feet as we splashed along to the northwest. The land here was barren, sustaining only a few miserable spatters of foliage here and there. It was a gloomy place, especially with the dark clouds still smothering everything in a dismal grey. In some spots, large depressions in the River bottom would drop down into a quick blackness, and we cautiously kept our distance. Our alligator count had reached over five hundred, and many of them had been bigger than our kayaks. With numbers that high, we were wary of splashing through any areas where we couldn't see the bottom.

We sloshed nearly half a mile through the dark, muddy waters before we found a deeper channel again. Our time back in the boats lasted only two miles or so, and then the River dried out even worse than before. It was hard not to get discouraged, but what could we do? Where could we go but north? It was the only way home now. We got out again and splashed on, both silently wondering but not daring to ask out loud if this would get worse before it got better.

Very slowly, our surroundings began to change as the day went on. The banks were still low, but now firm and grass covered. More and more grass seemed to stretch out ahead of us until finally we found ourselves amidst a rippling infinity of it on either side, a vast prairie as far as we could see. Then, just as suddenly as it had been swallowed up hours before, the sun reappeared, bathing everything in a bright, welcoming glow. The colors of the prairie were unleashed, bursting out in radiant greens and golds that reached to the horizon. A cool breeze swept up from the north, sending little ripples around my ankles as I stopped for a moment, taking it all in and smiling despite our circumstances.

The dark clouds had now moved on, and we continued our hike under a high sun, watching the River become narrower and narrower. Finally it shrunk to a mere trickle, gurgling inch-deep through the prairie in a channel so small I could have almost straddled both banks. Even under the new cheer of the warm sun I began to worry. Could the River actually dry up completely? Several people had told us that our way would get a little shallow, but this was getting ridiculous. There was almost nothing left of it!

"If we have to keep walking like this," David commented behind me, "we're never gonna cover our minimum distance for today."

I scanned the grasslands to my left and right, hoping for a moment that perhaps this was all just some mistake. Maybe somehow we got mixed up and the real River was somewhere else, flowing wide and deep like what we knew back home. But I quickly came back to my senses—it just wasn't true. There was no other way.

"We don't have a choice," I called back against the growing wind. "As long as there's still water, we've gotta keep going."

"And if we run out of water?"

I hesitated for a moment. "We still keep going."

David laughed. "I'm with ya, buddy," he assured me. "I'll keep going with ya even if we have to drag these boats across the whole prairie!"

"I know you would," I smiled. "That's why I'm glad you're the one who ended up coming with me."

A dark sliver suddenly appeared in the distance through the grass. We both saw it but continued forward in silence, not wanting to get our hopes up. As we came closer, however, I finally breathed a sigh of relief.

"Water!"

Only about a quarter mile ahead of us, our tiny path opened back up to form a deep channel once more. A small sandy peninsula jutted out there, and when we had arrived we pulled the kayaks up onto it and stopped for a well-earned food break. We picked out a few items for our early afternoon meal and ate sitting in the white sand, our feet submerged in the cool water as it rippled by.

"We can't sit around for too long," I managed to get out with a mouthful of crackers. "We've already lost a lot of time having to walk all that way."

"We should only have a few miles from here to Lake Winder," David said. "Hopefully it'll be smooth sailing."

"That lake's about a two-and-a-half-mile paddle from one side to the other," I reminded him. "It's not huge, but this wind might give us a little trouble."

"Hey, as long as there's water, I'm happy!"

After this point the River remained both deep and wide, and we had no problem traveling through. Within two miles it turned from the west and took a more northerly heading, and both banks were covered in ten-foot-high shoots of giant reed. Now when I say covered, I mean absolutely covered—they were so thick you couldn't see a thing through them. They were the deepest, richest gold I have ever seen, contrasting sharply with the striking cerulean sky. They blocked out the prairie, and we were enveloped in a calm silence; the only sound that could be heard was the gentle hissing of the tops of the stalks as they waved in the growing wind. Amid that secret beauty I felt all of the toils of the day disappear as if they had never been, and continued down our watery way in high spirits.

Within a half mile we left the golden reeds behind, and the banks took on a more barren, wind-swept look, rising a few feet on either side to obscure our view beyond them. Then with the turn of one last bend we were there, staring at the mouth of Lake Winder. We paddled straight for the open waters without hesitation, but as soon as we cleared the shelter of the riverbanks a determined northerly wind met us head-on. The blast took us by surprise, and seeing that the water was fairly rough, we decided to fall back and take one more quick break before tackling it. We rested and stretched for about five minutes on the last little nub of wind-worn land, then dutifully returned to the boats.

The wind made the crossing of Lake Winder a bit more taxing, but we were thankful to reach the other side without any major setbacks. The lake remained deep throughout, as did the River that met us again at the northeastern shore. From there, the River ran northeast for four more miles through another vast stretch of prairie, and finally to the shore of Lake Poinsett. As we closed in, however, things were not looking to be in our favor.

David's shoulder started to bother him, so we had to slow down a bit. It was already later in the afternoon, and the wind continued to grow in strength; by the time the River finally opened up to Lake Poinsett, it was whipping and howling in a deafening gale. The low sun was once more obscured by a scattered mass of clouds, giving the stormy waters beyond a sickly look of grey and green as they tossed and foamed. The very sight seemed to quench my courage.

I looked over at David, who was clearly in pain. "Let's stop here on the shore!" I shouted over the roar. "We'll take a little breather before we cross!"

We pulled up the kayaks to keep them from being blown away, grabbed a few things to eat, then collapsed on the battered grass. I dumped a big handful of granola into my mouth and could barely even hear the crunch as I chewed. David swallowed a pile of crackers with his right hand and with the left tried messaging his shoulder, wincing as he pushed at the spot.

"I'm hurting pretty bad, man!" he hollered.

I tried not to show the sense of dread that came over me as he said it. I was silent for a few moments, not wanting to ask, but finally I did.

"You think you can make it across this?"

Another few moments of silence.

David looked out in dismay for a moment at the five miles of raging open water that lay before us, then his face hardened. "I'll make it," he resolved. "I'll make it across one way or another!"

It was time. The two of us leaned into the wind as we returned to the boats, and I tried hard to quiet my better judgment as I pushed off and made my way with David out into Lake Poinsett.

It was terrible. I can say with confidence that it was the worst lake crossing I have ever done in my life, and I've done a lot. Our course through the lake ran east to west, but the wind was coming from the north, so those waves broadsided us the entire way. Neither the driving wind nor the pounding waves lightened for one moment the entire time we were out there. We fought with every paddle stroke for over two hours, taking only a few fleeting moments now and then to swallow a mouthful of water. We were constantly kept on our guard by some of the big waves that were breaking at random, threatening to dump their seething white crests into the boats.

We were cold and wet, not to mention exhausted, having already traveled over twenty miles that day. Every grueling moment seemed to pass by at a snail's pace, pulling at us, holding us back from the far shore. But I must include here that David stayed up with me the entire way, fighting through what must have been severe pain. He did not complain once, but instead focused all his strength and will on the task at hand. If he hadn't earned his salt before, he did that day.

I cannot express my relief when I noticed the western shore finally growing closer. The River once more reappeared, bending around to the north, and as we came back under the shelter of its banks the roaring wind and waves were hushed, and it was finally calm again.

We had only rounded the first bend when a long wood frame building with a shallow gable roof came into view ahead on our right. Its large deck stretched out over the River about ten feet above the water, and a wood plank dock was floating down at our level, only about six feet wide but running far beyond both the north and south sides of the building. A couple of airboats were bobbing lazily against it, and there was a small crowd of people outside. A giant bridge stretched high across the River just beyond it.

We mostly let our boats drift in with the current until they nudged up against the side of the dock. Tying them up, we rolled out onto the weathered grey boards and lay there for several minutes, utterly spent, staring up at the patches of dark blue sky through the clouds.

"We may still be able to end where we were supposed to today," I finally commented, staggering to my feet. "This should be Lone Cabbage Fish Camp. From here it should only be another seven and a half miles to the next bridge."

David didn't say anything for a moment, but then answered gravely, "I don't know if I can crank out another seven and a half today, brother; my shoulder's killing me." I had completely forgotten about his shoulder since we had started the crossing!

"You don't think there's any way you could pull it off? We're gonna have to make up that seven and a half at some point if we don't cover it today."

David thought hard, clenching his jaw and scratching silently at a knot in one of the wood planks. "I just...don't think I can do it."

I opened my mouth for another appeal but caught myself before the words came out. David was tough. Frozen nights, blazing heat, raging storms—we had faced it all together on past journeys. If he was saying his shoulder hurt bad enough to keep him from continuing, then he was really hurting. Disappointed but understanding, I agreed that we should stop there at Lone Cabbage for the night and give his shoulder some time to recover. We would start off first thing the next morning.

We trudged up the wooden ramp to the deck above in the late afternoon light, empty water jugs in hand. A husband and wife sat with their children at one of the wooden picnic tables, giving us strange looks as we went by. I tipped my hat and smiled, thinking of what we probably looked like after that long day. We found the door and stepped in.

The large, open space was empty and dimly lit. The western wall was mostly screened panels, though a few bugs had nevertheless found their way in and were frantically buzzing around the lights above. Ahead of us was a long bar that spanned nearly the entire width of the building, complete with a host of stools neatly spaced underneath, and just beyond that was a wood board wall with a door at either end. We would have thought that no one was inside but for the occasional clattering of metal utensils coming from behind them. The two of us hoisted ourselves up onto some stools, slumped over the bar, and waited patiently. It took a few minutes, but eventually a young blonde in her mid-twenties came out.

"Hey guys, how are ya?" she asked in a disinterested tone, then wrinkled her nose a bit in spite of herself as she actually looked up and took in our soaking, dirty frames. "What...uh...what can I get ya?"

"Ma'am, we're kayakers," I smiled politely. "We just crossed Lake Poinsett and we've still got a long ways to go...many more days, in fact. We've each drank one of our water jugs, and were wondering if it'd be too much trouble to fill them up."

I was surprised when the woman instantly shook her head. "Sorry guys, can't do that; it's against company policy. I can sell you bottled water and you can fill up your jugs with that."

"You mean, like, the little bottles?" David asked. "How much are they?"

"One seventy-five apiece."

"One seventy-five! Ma'am, it would take us over forty dollars to fill up these two jugs with those!"

"We're not talking about ice water with lemon or something," I tried again, "we just need water from a sink or even a hose if that's all you can spare." But she shook her head firmly again.

"It's against company policy."

David and I stared at each other in disbelief. I think it was the only time before or since when I'd ever heard the words "company policy" out on the River. I let it go and composed myself again.

"Okay, we certainly don't want to get anybody in trouble. We've got a couple other jugs; we'll just make those last. But we've got one more question, and this one is a bit more urgent. We meant to finish a bit farther north today, but my buddy here messed up his shoulder and we need dry ground to camp for the night. Could we please set up our tent on the grass out there? We would set up out of the way, and it would only be for tonight. We'll be gone before sunrise."

The woman's expression could not have been more indifferent as she once again shook her head unyieldingly. "Can't let you guys do that; it's against company policy."

"We're talking about a six-by-six patch of grass for the night," David's face grew red. "This whole stretch of the River is marshland! It's against company policy to let a couple of tired kayakers pitch their tent on a bit of dry ground for the night?"

"That's right." The woman remained emotionless. I was about to give up when I saw a moment of hesitation, then the slightest glimmer of curiosity cross her face. "Where you guys from, anyway?" I took the opportunity at once, hoping that maybe in sharing the story we could get her to bend company policy after all.

"We're a couple of kayakers from central Florida, just north of Lake Monroe; we put in down at Blue Cypress Lake two days ago. We're trying to make it to the Atlantic Ocean, so we've still got over two hundred miles to go."

Her eyes widened. "Are you guys insane?" Now, normally when people said that to us—and we did get that a lot—they would say it with a chuckling grin, but this woman was dead serious. "Do you know this River?" she pointed north.

"Well, we haven't been on this particular part of the River before," I started to explain, "but we're—"

"Then you *don't* know this River," she snapped. "There's folks that have lived here their whole lives, and they still get lost out there. There's no civilization for miles and miles once you pass here—no houses, no marinas, no roads save but a few overpasses with no access. Once you pass that," she pointed behind her again to the bridge looming in the waning light, "you're in no-man's-land. You guys are in for trouble if you try to get through that."

"Thanks for the advice," I replied with all the courtesy I could muster. As we got up from the barstools, I figured there was no harm in trying once more. "So...you're *sure* you can't let us camp here for the night? No fire. No noise. We just need a dry place to pitch our tent so we can sleep."

"Nope, it's against company policy."

We walked back outside as the sun was drawing close to the horizon through the ragged clouds. Our situation looked bleak. What if the woman was right? What if we *were* crazy? What if we really *did* get lost out there? I watched David straining as he massaged his shoulder—was going on even the right thing to do at this point? Maybe my own personal ambition was blinding me to my friend's need for help. Here we were, at the last point of access to the outside world for the next forty miles—was all this mess simply God trying to make it perfectly clear that we needed to call it quits? I suddenly realized that my teeth were chattering. A deep, inner chill was creeping in, and I knew I needed to get into some dry clothes.

"Hey, look over there!" David nudged me. I followed his pointing and could just make out a pitiful little patch of white sand on the far west side of the bridge. "It's not much," he grinned, "but it looks like there might be enough space for the tent."

I hesitated. "I don't know, man...do you think we should just...I mean, we're each down a water jug, we don't know if that spot out there is actually dry, your shoulder is killing you, and we've got all that distance waiting for us first thing tomorrow. I just don't know…maybe we need to—"

David slapped his hand on my shoulder and gripped it tightly. He knew what I was thinking. He looked me straight in the eye. "Daniel, I'm not gonna lie to ya, I'm hurtin', but I'm not done. I'm not gonna give up this easy. Let's just take a look at that spot over there; hopefully it'll work. If it does, let's leave tomorrow for tomorrow and get as much rest as we can."

I pursed my lips and tried to clench my chattering teeth for a moment, thinking it over. My eyes went from David to the sandy spot by the bridge behind him, then back to David. "Okay," I resolved slowly, "if you're still willing, let's do it."

As we headed for the ramp that led back down to the dock, a lean grey-haired man greeted us. "Howdy boys! Where you off to?"

"Well, they wouldn't let us camp here," David shrugged, "so we're heading to that spot over there on the other side of the bridge. Tomorrow we're heading north."

"Sir, do you know anything about the area just north of here?" I decided to ask.

"Oh ya, I've gone through there a bunch of times."

"Is it hard to find your way through?"

He wrinkled his nose as he thought. "It's probably not too bad right now because the water's so low; lots of those other channels oughta be dried up, so you've at least got less choices! You can still get lost pretty easy, though. The best thing to do is just follow the current. Wherever it goes, that's where you should go. Ya'll remember that and you'll be okay."

I was a little relieved by his casual response. "Do you think the main channel might be dried up in places as well, or should we be able to get kayaks through?"

"Nah, you oughta be okay depth-wise…it's just a long way."

"We know!" David laughed. "Thank you, sir!"

That sandy spot turned out to be just big enough to pitch the tent, leaving us only a couple feet from the water's edge. We set up the boats like a wall between us and the shoreline, hoping to shield ourselves from curious alligators or the wake of any passing airboats during the night. It was the best we could do; the sun had already set, and the last light of day was fading.

The clouds had cleared once more, and stars shone clean and bright in the darkening sky. A cool breeze swept in through the mesh roof above us as I zipped myself snugly into my sleeping bag, having finally swapped into some dry clothes. Crickets took up their enchanting lullaby as the very last streaks of violet fell into the horizon, singing of a time before cars and bridges...before company policy.

"How's your arm?" I asked quietly as David climbed into his sleeping bag.

He moved it a little bit. "Really sore."

I paused for a moment, then, "Do you really think you can go on, man?" The silence that followed in the dark wasn't comforting.

"I'm...just gonna push through it, that's all."

"David, you're not gonna just push through a minimum of thirty-six miles with a shoulder like that. Any distance we can't cover tomorrow is gonna get stacked on top of the seven-and-a-half-mile deficit we already have. We're at a critical point right now. Every stopping point on the entire trip will need to be changed if we can't somehow make up today's lost distance. If we can't make it up, we're gonna miss the Jolly Gator Fish Camp tomorrow night, which will mean another day of not being able to replenish our water. Even worse, we won't be able to stop at your place two nights from now. We'll have to pass it by."

I heard David give a long sigh. "Let me sleep on it. We'll set the alarm for 6:00 tomorrow so we can be on our way before sunrise. If my shoulder isn't any better by then...well...I guess we'll figure that out when the time comes."

My stomach churned. I was dreading the next day, fairly certain that it would see the end of our journey. If David couldn't go on, I would need to help him figure out how to get home. By the time help came to this remote place, more than half the day could already be lost. And even then, did I really have the courage to go on alone? I grabbed my small flashlight and opened Nicole's second letter.

Is it everything you imagined? I hope so! I know you must be tired, but probably still excited. I hope you had a great day today. Stay strong!

I turned off the light and laid on my back, looking up at the stars through the mesh as my eyes grew heavy. I whispered as a prayer the words from the old hymn as I drifted off to sleep:

Jesus, Savior, pilot me
Over life's tempestuous sea
Unknown waves before me roll
Hidden rock and treacherous shoal
Chart and compass come from Thee
Jesus, Savior, pilot me

THROUGH THE LABYRINTH

"Yeah, I know it's crazy, but I feel fine!" David was rotating his shoulder around in the darkness of the early morning. "It's never just stopped hurting like this!"

I was excited but hesitant, finding it hard to believe. "You sure you're okay to keep going? There are a lot of miles between us and the Jolly Gator, and there's no help out there."

"No man, really, I feel completely fine!" David smiled as he stretched contentedly, then reached into his food bag for something to eat. "Let's get moving as quick as we can."

We did. By 6:30 we had packed everything and were pushing out onto the water. The waning gibbous moon was still high in the sky, its pale glow exposing the lonely, lifeless silhouette of Lone Cabbage Fish Camp. Hushed silence still hung over the world, and even the soft dips of our paddle blades seemed like breaking glass in the calm. A faint white mist lay like a blanket around us, swirling as we cut through.

It felt unreal to be heading out like normal again; I had been almost certain the night before that David's shoulder would be the end of our journey. I kept expecting to wake up from a dream and find myself back in the tent, but it wasn't a dream. David was cruising effortlessly through the mist beside me, taking in long deep breaths of the cool morning air with no evidence of pain. I whispered a prayer of thanks with a smile.

It was only a matter of minutes before the River forked into two channels, one to the east and the other to the west, and for a moment we hesitated. There had been no good navigational charts for the section ahead. Here the River splintered into a maze of smaller channels that snaked and criss-crossed their way through a vast flood plain. I had spent hours trying to guess the best way through using old satellite pictures, but I was still more unsure about our course for that day than any other. During the planning of the trip, David and I had taken to calling this stretch the Southern Labyrinth.

"This is it," David observed in a hushed voice. "I'd be lying if I said I wasn't nervous. You sure you can find the way through?"

"Ask me this afternoon and I'll give you a more accurate answer," I smirked, pulling out my hand-drawn map protected within two layers of plastic bags. "The only way we're gonna know if this thing was worth the trouble is by trying it out." We each grabbed a swig of water, then humbly took up our paddles and followed the western channel into the Southern Labyrinth.

What small trees there were on the banks quickly vanished, and even in the dark I could sense a wide-open expanse stretching out on either side of us. I felt serious as we went along in silence; maybe it was the recognition of our own insignificance and helplessness in that enormous place. We had already covered several miles by the time the grey of the approaching dawn began to slowly soak up the starry night sky.

"It's chilly right now," David whispered as he watched, "but I'll bet that sun'll heat things up real quick, especially with no trees out here."

I agreed, then added, "Current's pretty good here. If we can keep going at this speed, we should be able to take a good chunk out of today's mileage before the sun gets too high."

We continued in reverent silence once more. I began to hear the songs of waking birds out in the lonely darkness of the prairie, greeting the brightening grey that continued to creep up from the horizon. The dark melted to violet, and the violet gave way to fiery red. It slowly bled through the entire sky, illuminating it from the still dark earth, and I gasped as I was finally able to take in the true enormity of our surroundings. There was nothing in any direction to obscure the line of the horizon; it surrounded us in a full, unbroken circle—no trees, no buildings, nothing. I watched as the fire reds were soaked with orange before my eyes, creeping their way overhead and all the way to the far west. The colors blended and deepened, spreading out over us like some unbelievably vast dome with endless layers, moving through the unbroken sky as the warm gold of true sunlight began to appear.

I had never seen such a big sky before. I felt so small, just a mere speck accidentally caught up in that enveloping triumph of dawn. I felt a tear run down my face, but I didn't even bother to wipe it off. I found myself silently mouthing the words of the Psalmist,

When I look at your heavens, the work of your fingers,
The moon and the stars, which you have set in place,
What is man that you are mindful of him,
And the son of man that you care for him?

The dark landscape around us burst into a lush prairie, blazing green and gold under the new sun. Great herds of cattle, which until then had been hidden in the darkness, suddenly appeared all around us hundreds strong, rousing themselves to graze. An old black bull by the River's edge bellowed and tossed his horned head at us as we passed, but was too intent on breakfast to take any further action. I found myself drawn to the unique beauty of that place in the growing light. If it were possible for a place to be honest or straightforward, it would have been that place. There were no secrets, just a simple openness...and yet somehow at the same time so much more than I could take in.

For once, the extremely low water levels worked to our advantage. As the man at Lone Cabbage had predicted, most of the superfluous channels were completely dried up, usually leaving only one obvious channel to follow. Without any difficult decisions to make concerning our route, we were able to quickly cover much more distance than I had expected. I kept fearing that the wind might pick up as it had the day before; with absolutely nothing to buffer it, it would be able to rip through that place and really give us trouble. But it never came. Only a cool, steady breeze whispered through the grass as we continued north.

Before noon we had completed nearly half our mileage for the day, and I knew we would soon reach Cone Lake. It was barely more than a mile at its longest point, but had a strange feature: the River's banks jutted far out into it's middle. The River continued at the northeast corner of the lake, so by the time we actually cleared the riverbanks into Cone Lake we would have already overshot our exit; in fact, it would add an extra three-quarters of a mile to follow the water for this maneuver. Instead, I planned to simply pull our kayaks over the narrow bank and make a straight shot for the northern shore, saving ourselves both distance and time. It seemed like a good idea...until we reached the spot.

The shore sloped up a couple of feet on each side of us, obscuring our view of what was beyond, so I climbed out of Old Orange to have a look. As I cleared the top, my heart sank. Stretched out between us and the shallow water in the distance was about three hundred yards of slimy black muck—leftovers of what had been the lake bottom.

"Oh wow, that got dried up pretty good," David muttered as he climbed up beside me.

"Well," I sighed, "there's no way we can haul the boats through that. We'll just have to take the long way out into the middle of the lake." We both tried to look west, but a mess of tall reeds obstructed our view.

"Hopefully there still *is* a lake," David muttered. "The view doesn't look too promising from here."

The transition into Cone Lake was hardly noticeable; the lake had dried up so much that it was not much wider than the River itself. There was one big difference, however, which we noticed immediately.

"Oh no, I'm bottoming out!"

As soon as David said it I felt it, too. It wasn't the grainy scratching of a hard, sandy bottom, but rather the sliding squish of loose black muck. Within moments my speed slowed to a crawl and finally to a silent halt. I tried a few paddle strokes, but they barely did anything—it was like trying to move through glue. I took a few more strokes, straining as I pulled back with everything I had, pushing up piles of muck above the surface as I dug in. Old Orange made a little scoot forward, maybe a couple inches, then stuck fast.

As I stopped struggling and paused to think, I became aware of the empty silence—no planes, no cars or lawnmowers in the distance, nothing but the hush of that gentle northern breeze. I looked around, trying to think of any other options we had to get to the other side of that lake, but there was nothing for it. Muck or no muck, our only hope was to push through.

"We're just gonna have to manhandle this."

"Yup," David sighed, "I was afraid of that. Well, let's get this over with!"

The water was barely a film over the top, so paddling is really not the word to use for what we did—we were more just pushing. The putrid smell of sulfur rose around us as we sloshed about, and it wasn't long before both we and the boats were covered in the stinking black spatter. Still we shoved on, determined to make it out. My arms and shoulders began to burn from the strain, and my shirt stuck to my back as sweat trickled down. I looked behind and could see a trail of congealed slime on either side of my thick skid mark—inch by inch we were making progress.

It was grueling work, but fortunately it was a small lake, and after about a half hour of mud bogging the water finally began to deepen. We reached the River once more at the northeastern corner of Cone Lake, and to our relief the route was uneventful, meandering back and forth through an easily navigable channel. We traveled for another hour before we suddenly happened upon a Timucuan shell mound that was not on the map. The foot of its enormous bulk met the west bank in a beautiful sandy beach, but as it rose away from the water its face was covered with a dense stand of palms, maples, sweetgums, and oaks, which cast a cool shade over the ancient hill in the midafternoon light. The mound climbed to roughly twenty feet, and the topmost of those trees almost seemed to rise up like spires of a great fortress or a royal crown.

David smiled as he looked. "I know we've gotta keep moving, but I think this place would be worth a stop."

"I agree. Let's take a quick break to get some food and then we'll start up again."

I jumped into the shallows and hauled Old Orange up onto the warm white sand. Everywhere the beach was littered with weathered white shells and auburn bits of archaic pottery, and only several yards further up the dancing shadows of the trees played against them. The whole mound seemed to be alive, rippling green and silver in the breeze. I breathed in deep, trying hard to take in the beauty of this ancient way-stop in the precious few minutes we had there.

We ate reclining by the shore in the cool shade, feet in the sand, for as long as we could possibly justify it. Neither of us wanted to leave, but there were still many more miles left to cover for the day. Refreshed from our short stop, we stowed our bags, shoved the boats back out into the River, and continued on in the steady current. We had not gone very far past the mound when shallow swaths of sandbars appeared, and we were forced to get out and walk the kayaks several times, though only for short distances. After only about half a mile of these setbacks, we found ourselves back in deep water.

"Alright," David slapped the side of New Blue, "we've got our depth back. Let's make up that lost time!"

But he spoke too soon. As we turned the very next bend, we were met by a terrible surprise: the River was gone. Now, when I say gone, I don't mean it was too shallow or that it had dried into muck, I mean it was *completely gone*—the water simply ended in a high grassy bank.

"Uh...are you sure this is the way?" David asked after a few moments of silence. "You've got that map right-side up, right?"

I beached Old Orange and climbed up the rise to get a look. I could just make out a body of water far out on the prairie, but it seemed to be just an isolated pond. Or was it? I couldn't see well enough to be sure. I looked up at the sun, now well past its zenith and casting lengthening shadows in the waving grass, and my stomach began to churn as I realized we were lost. I had no idea where we were or where we had gone off course; I couldn't even remember seeing an alternate channel for miles.

I looked back toward the north at the narrow strip of water in the distance. We could try hauling the boats over and see if we could find a channel that would get us back on track, but just getting over there would take a considerable amount of time. If no way out could be found, we would just have to drag them all the way back and start over. By then, we would have lost much of the daylight we had left and would be forced to camp out on the prairie. But, then again, what if that bit of water really was the way, and we were able to find a way through? What if it was the *only* way?

I bit my lip and twisted the hairs on my chin, paralyzed with indecision—we were running out of time. I checked the map once more. If we backtracked for a few miles, it looked like there might be an alternate route besides the one we had been following, but a good chunk of that route extended beyond the view of the map; it was too risky to simply hope that the unseen chunk was navigable. Then I remembered the advice of the man we had met back at Lone Cabbage: Follow the current.

"Of course!" I said out loud, slapping myself in the head for forgetting the simplest navigational trick in the book.

"What?" David asked, confused.

I jumped back into Old Orange. "Come on, let's go back for just a bit and see if we passed any other channels."

"I don't remember seeing any."

"Me neither, but there was definitely a current just a little ways back and now it's stagnant. If there was a current, the water had to have been moving somewhere."

We made our way back, and within only a few minutes we noticed a small creek forking off from the larger channel, so small that neither of us had noticed it as we had gone by.

"Do you think that could...?" David muttered.

I scraped off a dried patch of sand from the side of Old Orange and sprinkled it into the water, holding my breath. Sure enough, the scattered white grains were quickly swept away northward as they sunk into the dark.

"This must be it!" I announced.

"Doesn't look like much."

"No it doesn't, but there's definitely a current running through it."

David's eyes narrowed. "How can this little dinky thing be the right way? What if we follow it a good ways only to have it empty into a slough or something?"

I threw up my hands. "What else can we do? If we've got a current, I say let's see where it goes. If we hit another roadblock, we'll just have to tackle it when we get to it."

"Alright," David shrugged, "let's see what happens!"

The creek was small, but to my surprise it remained just deep enough for us to paddle through. After another half hour it emptied into a wide channel, and it became obvious that we had made the right choice after all and were back on track. The current even seemed to pick up a little as if it understood we were running short on time, but now I knew for sure that we would not beat the sun to the Jolly Gator Fish Camp. The land was now covered with long, lazy shadows as the sun drew close to the horizon.

"We're not gonna make it," I called over to David. "We just don't have enough time."

"How much farther do we have to get to the Jolly Gator?"

"We're almost exactly as short today as we were yesterday, about seven and a half miles. We should probably start looking for some level ground for the tent while we've still got a bit of light left."

David thought silently for a few moments. "So if we can reach the Jolly Gator tonight, we'd be able to stay at my place tomorrow night, right?"

"Well, yeah. From the Jolly Gator it'd be around thirty-something miles to your place, but the Jolly Gator is still seven and a half miles away." I started scanning the shore for a good stopping point. With all the cattle we had seen that day, hopefully they wouldn't get too curious and crush us during the night.

"Let's go for it."

"What?"

"Let's go for it!" David repeated. "I'll go through the night if you will! We can make the Jolly Gator tonight, and that'll put us back on schedule to land at my place tomorrow."

"No way, buddy. A big chunk of that seven and a half miles is through Puzzle Lake—they don't call it that for nothing! Right now we at least have enough light to find a decent campsite. If we go through Puzzle Lake at night and get lost, we could end up in the middle of a slough."

"We'll make it!" David smiled confidently. "I know we can make it!"

I hesitated before answering. "If we go, we've got to haul. Can your shoulder handle all this distance?"

David nodded. "I'll match you mile for mile."

"Then I guess that's settled. Jolly Gator, here we come!"

It took a few minutes to find the headlamps in the dimming light, but I finally managed to pull them both out of my dry bag. I tossed one to David, we both fitted them securely onto our hats, and David mounted Jay's old GPS to the gunnel of New Blue.

Now, let me remind the reader—especially younger ones—that this was 2009, and Jay had already owned this particular GPS unit for several years. It was little more than a bulky yellow box with a postage stamp-sized LCD screen, which was blank except for some coordinate points I had preloaded from a computer back home. There was no map overlay to check against, and even the dim orange backlight wouldn't stay on for more than five seconds at a time! However, if you haven't realized it by now, this was not exactly a lavishly funded expedition to start with; it was the best we could do with what we had. Since the GPS points I had created were based on outdated satellite maps, their reliability was questionable. Still, I figured that just about anything was better than traveling completely blind. If the GPS points proved to be wrong, we would decide what to do when the time came.

David shone his headlamp at the screen and squinted. "Looks like we're around point A...A194? Does that sound familiar?"

"Yup, just keep calling the points out to me as we pass them. I spent so much time running through the route that it should at least give me a bit of a reference point. Let's go!"

The air was still now, quietly reverent as the dying red sun fell into the horizon; I felt the temperature drop as it happened. Depth slowly dissolved to vague grey, and ultimately the landscape degraded into a flat silhouette before our eyes. As the last light gave way to a moonless indigo, I could see the dim ice blue of Venus appear low in the west. The indigo went to navy, and the navy gave way to true black. Stars began to emerge, first here and there, then quickly by the hundreds.

The sky, rather than darkening, now grew in brightness as innumerable stars began blazing out unhindered, and the pale band of the Milky Way soaked through. It no longer seemed black at all but rather clear; there was no barrier between us and the deep heavens. The water around us lost its distinction from the sky, taking on its same translucent, infinite depth, and the dips of my paddle seemed to ripple space and time. I felt like I was traveling at impossible speeds—surely we had left earth behind.

"We're coming up on A200," David's voice jolted me back to the task at hand, "about three hundred yards."

I ran through the map in my head. "I think we're closing in on Puzzle Lake."

"That's good then, right?"

"We'll see, I guess!"

Suddenly I heard a small disturbance, followed by a splash a moment later. I flicked my light on and turned to the sound, but all I caught was a crown of ripples dancing upon the glassy water. I turned it back off, but then the sound came again, a little closer. Then it came again.

"What is that?" David wondered.

My headlamp came on again just in time to see a fish leap out of the water right in front of me, fly over the boat, and plunge into the blackness on the other side.

"The fish are jumping!" I laughed. "Don't let them whack you in the face!"

The odd acrobatics show continued for several minutes as we closed in on Puzzle Lake. I cannot tell you exactly when we got there or what it looked like, because we couldn't see any of it! The channel seemed to broaden only a little, but we could have merely been in one small portion of the lake, hemmed in by strips of marsh grasses in the shallow water.

Surprisingly, the GPS points seemed to be fairly accurate. We ran aground in some shallow water only a handful of times, and the errors were always minor and easily correctable. Finally, I spied the far away lights of a bridge toward the north, streaking here and there through the tangled reeds.

"Don't get too excited," I warned David as I pointed it out. "Remember that in this place there are no trees, nothing to block our line of sight. It looks close, but depending on where this maze takes us it could still be hours before we reach it."

"It's still encouraging, though. Nothing's gonna stop me from getting there now that I can see it!"

I hesitated to agree out loud. Over the years I had seen how quickly good progress could grind to a halt with the turn of a bend, and I certainly didn't want to be caught unawares. I stayed cautious, peering as best I could into the disorienting mosaic of reflected stars and cryptic swaths of black before us.

It was nearly another hour of winding through the darkness before David called out, "A212!"

"That's the point I've been waiting for," I told him. "We should be getting near the end of Puzzle Lake now. Only a couple of miles left until the Jolly Gator!"

We both picked up the pace. By this point the air was damp and cold and we were weary from the long day, but ahead the bridge was now truly close; the hazy yellow lights gleaming across its length seemed to make the whole thing glow. I knew that just on the other side of that bridge, though it was obscured from view, the Jolly Gator was waiting for us. Once more we hit a dead end but quickly recovered, having just veered a little too far towards the western shore. We rounded the bend, all the dark clutter fell away, and we were suddenly bathed in the light of the bridge, now looming just ahead of us across clear open water. A small white block building sat dimly lit on the grassy hill just beyond it.

"We made it!" David shouted with excitement. "It's the Jolly Gator!"

I collapsed into my seat and laughed with relief—we were back on schedule. Not only would we be staying at the Jolly Gator that night, but if all went well we would be at Jay's house tomorrow. We quickly made our way through the concrete pylons of the bridge and were soon staring up at the old fish camp. The lights were off inside, and there were no cars or boats in sight.

"What time is it, anyway?" I asked David as he coasted up beside me.

He shrugged. "Beats me. I think it's pretty safe to say that they're gone for the night, though."

I was disappointed—though not completely surprised—that the place was empty. On several of our trips in the early days, Roger and Howard had let us stay there and given us dinner on the house. My mouth watered as I recalled the heaping baskets of fried gator nuggets they would bring out for us! It had been a couple of years since we had last seen them, and I had been hoping to tell them about our adventures.

"I guess it's for the best," I decided out loud. "If they were here we'd probably end up talking for another hour, and we really need to get some sleep after a day like this!"

We passed the hill, veered west into the small canal that wrapped around its north side, and finally brought the boats to a halt against the sandy shore. I jumped out onto land and suddenly shivered. Warm against my seat all that time, I hadn't noticed just how cold the air had become; now the sweat that had been soaking the back of my shirt instantly began to chill me as I looked around. It was all much the same as I remembered it from years ago, though the empty night made it feel more lonely than on previous visits. A damp, clinging fog was rolling in quickly from the east.

"Let's get the tent set up and get ready for bed," David advised. "We've got a long day ahead of us tomorrow."

My teeth were chattering violently by the time we were crawling into the tent, and it was a blessed relief to finally sink into a warm sleeping bag. It was well past ten o'clock, and we had traveled roughly forty-two miles. We had done it—we had made it through the Southern Labyrinth.

I heard David straining in his sleeping bag, then a burst of muffled flatulence. "Instant warmth!" he smiled.

I buried my face from the aftermath I knew would soon follow, my eyelids already heavy. "Good job today, buddy. I still can't quite believe we're actually here!"

"Ya, same," David stretched out his hands behind his head. "What time do you wanna wake up tomorrow?"

"Do you have a preference?"

"The sooner the better, man. I want to get home as soon as we can!"

"Alright...what do you say to 4:30?"

"Sounds good to me!"

"You sure you can get up that early?"

"Absolutely," David replied confidently. "If it was the only way to stay at home for a night, I'd pack up and leave right now if I had to!"

"Okay then, I'll see you at 4:30, buddy."

I was completely exhausted, but the thrill of being back on track and within range of our home base kept me hopeful despite my sore muscles. My eyes closed, and I drifted off almost immediately as the song of crickets pierced through the gathering fog.

A FAMILIAR WAY

"Alright dude, let's get moving," I shook David once more, but he didn't move. "Hey, it's 4:30, let's go!"

"Too early," David mumbled, cocooned inside his sleeping bag. "Just give me a little more sleep."

I grumbled loudly, knowing this would happen, but set the alarm for a little later. I crawled into my sleeping bag and instantly fell back to sleep.

The alarm went off once more: 5:00. I jumped into action and gave David a more forceful shove this time. "Get up man, we need to get a move on!" This time, with obvious reluctance, David managed to force himself up to a sitting position and slowly came to life.

"Wow, it's cold!" his tired voice cracked as he made the observation. He squinted at the wall of the tent closest to him, then reached out and touched it. "Ah, the tent's wet! That fog must have soaked it all night!"

I was already rolling up my sleeping bag. "Doesn't matter. We'll pack it wet and hopefully get home in time to dry it out. Regardless, there's nothing we can do about it now." David's face lit up at my mentioning home, and he joined me in packing.

We ate a quick breakfast, stowed our gear, and finally took down the tent. The fog still hung thickly in the air, making the cold that much more penetrating. My wet feet were numb and my teeth were chattering as we packed the last of the tent poles and set the whole bundle in its place. Old Orange's seat was completely soaked as the tent had been, so I grabbed an unused garbage bag among the gear and set it on top to keep my backside dry. I climbed in, pushed off, and joined David on the glassy water.

Fresh blisters stung on my palms and fingers for the first couple of paddle strokes, but the pain quickly subsided. Stars were still shining brightly, and the moon must have just risen above the horizon a couple hours earlier; the fog was illuminated by its pale glow as we made our way back out into the main channel. The Jolly Gator disappeared behind us, and in only a short time we covered the distance to Lake Harney. We couldn't see the lake itself because of the fog, but I could feel the shift in the air from close banks to open water, and harmless little waves began lapping at our bows. We stopped to grab one last snack before the crossing.

"How's the shoulder?" I asked as I munched some granola.

"It's fine," David assured me. "This cold is actually waking me up pretty good, and I feel ready to go!"

"Let's try to stick close together on this," I advised. "Visibility is pretty low out here. You still got your headlamp?"

A flash momentarily blinded me as David confirmed.

"Good. We'll try to make it to the other side by sunup."

David nodded and shoved the last of his fruit bar into his mouth. "Let's do it!"

The crossing was beautiful. Though we couldn't see much around us, the dark blues and violets of the starlit night were dancing on the quiet water. There was a cold breeze from the north, but as David had already commented, this morning it was a refreshing cold; I felt fully alert despite my lack of sleep from the night before. The muscles in my back were sore, but quickly warmed up with the paddling. Awash in the deep shades and night shadows, our boats created almost no wake, gliding soundlessly through the stars. It felt like flying more than anything.

It seemed like we stayed in this dream for hours until the light of a coming dawn began to gently soak the horizon with a pale grey glow. As the light continued to grow I spotted the far shore through a break in the fog, no more than a mile away. But then, suddenly, dawn was swallowed up in a thick blanket of unfriendly dark clouds which came sweeping in from the east. They quickly covered the entire sky. Consequently, the fog continued to lay thick across the surface of the water unchecked, and it was in this gloom that we finally reached Lake Harney's northern shore and returned to the River.

At this point there was no more uncertainty; we had traveled this section of the River many times and knew it well. From Lake Harney, the River gently bends to the northwest for about seven miles, then dips south for another three or so. At the end of this southward dip the River skirts by Mullet Lake, one of the campsites we had often used as a stopping point in the early days. David and I made it to this point without incident. The dark clouds began to unleash dense columns of heavy rain, but fortunately the northern breeze had blown the heart of it just south of us, and we were able to remain completely dry.

As we passed by Mullet Lake, I added up the rough distance in my head and frowned. "We're not doing so great. We've still got another eight miles or so to Lake Monroe, then another thirteen miles to get home. At the pace we're going, we're not going to make it before nightfall."

David's face wrinkled as he thought. "What about Snake Creek Pass? We used that a couple of times in the old days to shave off a little distance. That'd take us up by Thorn Hill Lake and put us out by the Vanishing Isles."

"Too risky. That pass has always been shallow, so who knows what it'd be like now with the water so low. We can't take the chance of getting stuck in there."

"So we'll just go through the night again like we did last night."

"We can't, man. We already lost a good amount of sleep pulling that forty-two miles yesterday, and I don't know about you, but I'm definitely starting to feel it." David's silence admitted the same. As much as I hated to push him with the possibility of his shoulder flaring up again, we had to face the facts. "If we keep running through the night and losing sleep with the distances we're covering, we're gonna crash. The way I see it, we've got two choices. We can either pick a spot further south to spend the night, or we've gotta pick up the pace to close the gap between us and home before sunset."

David was silent for a while, but then smiled. "Then let's get moving!" I wasted no time in increasing speed, and David matched me.

From there, the River kept a fairly westerly course for another six or seven miles, dipping south a bit to graze the northern shore of Lake Jesup and then swinging back up.

"See, look at that!" I pointed as the far end of Snake Creek Pass came into view. Instead of a channel, a slough of black muck ran as far back as we could see.

"Okay, good call on that one, buddy!" David laughed, clearly relieved to know that we really had chosen the best way after all.

We made our way through the Vanishing Isles, a small maze of low, reed-covered islands spanning roughly two miles. Typically they were submerged, with only tall reeds fluttering above the surface, but with the water level so low their gnarled black shores jutted out prominently, clearly defining our route through them. Little more than half a mile west of the Isles, the River funneled into a perfectly straight northwest channel, running roughly a mile until it met open water at the other end.

"The Monroe Canal," David recognized it with a raspy voice. "How are we doing on time?"

I took a moment to lean forward and stretch out my shoulders, which were beginning to tense up. "It's hard to say how we're doing until we're on the other side of Lake Monroe; there's no telling what's waiting for us at the other end of this canal. Could be that there's smooth waters and we make it across in an hour or two. Or could be that there's huge waves out there and we won't reach the other end until close to nightfall. More than likely it'll be somewhere in between. How you holding up?"

"I just wanna get home for a night," David confessed. "I'll hurt once we get there."

Monroe's mood was, as I had guessed, somewhere in the middle. A steady north wind blew against our right sides—we were traveling from east to west—and we were jostled a good bit from the waves, but it was nothing that was beyond our skill. It seemed to take forever to get across, but seeing as it was over five miles from one end to the other, that was usually the case. Even from the eastern shore you can clearly see the bridge that spans its far western point where it meets the River again. It seems deceptively close and so easy to reach, but for a long, long time it never seems to get any closer. Even after crossing the lake many times, it still always played with my resolve.

We finally reached the other side by early afternoon, though completely exhausted. I wanted nothing more than to just stop right under the pylons of the bridge and sleep for a week, and I knew David felt the same way. But we had just passed the last great obstacle between us and home, and nothing was going to stop us now. We swallowed some water from our jugs—we were almost out—and continued on, returning to our determined pace in an instant. From that point we knew every landmark, every turn of the River by heart.

We paddled hard for another three hours, and finally came upon the final stretch—I honestly couldn't believe it. We veered east off the main River through the narrow channel, and as we rounded the final bend Jay's dock came into view.

"We made it!" David laughed with relief.

We reached the shore at just about 5:00, making much better time than we expected, and within minutes I saw Jay and the family coming down from the house to meet us. He waved and quickly helped us unload our gear onto the grass.

"I'm going to be honest," he smiled as I handed him my blue dry bag, "I had my doubts as to whether you guys could make it or not. I'm pretty impressed!" He helped each of us up onto land and slapped us on the back.

Before anything else we made sure to set up the tent, which was still soaked from that morning, hoping that the last couple hours of sunlight would be enough to dry it out before bedtime. As we finished, I looked out at the familiar view of the two small islands which separated us from the sparkling River beyond. It felt odd. Nearly all of our trips had ended here in the past, but this time it was only a rough halfway point. I was conflicted as I thought on it; half of me felt like we had reached a successful end, and the other half knew that, come morning, we would be leaving home once again.

What temporarily took my mind off of this was the announcement that there was a dinner waiting for us—a real, cooked, homemade dinner! As I walked into the house, the familiar smells of the old fireplace and comfortably-aged cedar met me—it seemed like a year ago since I had been there. Jay, his wife Lauryn, his two daughters Jessica and Emily, and David and I all crowded around the dinner table over a steaming hot pan of lasagna, a heaping bowl of caesar salad, and a basket full of garlic bread. David and I ate as much as we could possibly get down, the whole time doing our best to answer questions and tell stories in between mouthfuls.

"The rest of the trip is going to be cake compared to that third day!" David laughed. "Forty-two miles—there's no way it could get worse than that!"

"Don't be so sure," Jay replied, taking a sip of his evening coffee. "You won't know what your hardest day was until you're standing on that beach looking out over the ocean."

I nodded in agreement. "You never know what's gonna be there to meet you around the next bend."

I genuinely tried so hard to make that night last, talking and laughing and eating with familiar faces. But the harder I tried, the faster time seemed to go; the entire evening seemed like a blur. Before I knew it the windows were dark, and I was struggling to keep my eyes open. It was time for bed.

Fortunately, the tent had dried completely by the time the sun had set, and I dragged myself in, eager to get some sleep. I knew that David was on his way, and had planned on waiting for him to get there to talk over the next morning, but as soon as I stopped moving I was gone.

A CHANGE OF PLANS

The woods around us were silent. A thick, impenetrable fog was on the water, so thick that even the end of the dock was only a weak silhouette against the misty white. It must have rolled in some time during the night, but somehow the tent had stayed fairly dry. It was now loaded securely in the bow of New Blue. It was 7:00, and we were once again ready to leave.

Jay and the family had woken up early to see us off, but now that everything was packed we all stood in an awkward silence on the shore. I knew David was fighting hard against the desire to stay—I felt it, too. As we stood there, tired and cold in the chilly darkness, heavy with the weight of so many days and miles before us, the journey truly seemed impossible. I figured Jay could see the struggle on our faces, but none of us dared to speak it out loud. I think we all understood just how fragile our wills were in that moment; one well-worded excuse might have broken us and ended our journey right then and there.

Jay gave me a knowing smile and nodded silently.

I took in a deep breath. "Well, this is it. Thanks for dinner last night, Lauryn!"

David and I went down the line, giving hugs to everyone, and without any further hesitation forced ourselves back into those two waiting boats. My blisters burned anew as I gave one good push with my paddle and coasted backward into the dark, foggy water.

Jay followed us to the end of the dock. "We'll see you at the beach!" he grinned as he waved. "You guys be careful, now!"

"We will!" David and I shouted back in unison, and with that we charged forward, home vanishing quickly behind us in the mist.

It didn't take long for my sense of adventure to resurface, and by the time we had covered the short distance back to the main channel of the River I felt like myself again. We stuck within sight of the eastern shore, not wanting a collision with a passing boat in the low visibility. We were only a few miles past Goat Island when I picked up on an odd noise. David heard it, too. We stopped paddling and listened intently. It sounded like rowing, but much louder and stronger than a typical boat. It was getting closer.

"A racing scull!" I shouted over to David, "It's gotta be!"

"Out on the River?"

Sure enough, within a few moments the long, narrow shadow appeared in the fog. It was a big one with eight rowers, though the whole thing was so streamlined that it was barely wider than Old Orange. As it neared us, the rowers stopped in unison and drew up their oars. It coasted up to us and the crew finally became visible through the veils of white. They were...girls!

I tried to hide my surprise as I tipped my hat to them. "Morning, ladies. Where ya heading?"

"We're just out practicing," the coxswain replied, adjusting her blonde ponytail.

"How fast can you go in that thing?" David asked, coming up next to me.

"Fast," one of the girls smirked.

"Are you heading back north, now?" I asked, and they nodded. "Well that's the same way we're heading, too—wanna have a little race?"

Several of the girls burst into laughter at the proposition and whispered to their companions, but finally replied, "Sure, why not?"

We positioned our boats side by side in the silent water. Even in the heavy fog, I could discern the dim glow of morning toward the east. The temperature was rising, and I wiped away a bead of sweat from my forehead as the girls dipped their oars in the water. The coxswain gave the order and we all burst into full speed. I ripped through the water with all the strength I had, jerking up the bow of Old Orange. But I seemed to be standing still, just sloshing around in the water compared to the unbelievable speed the scull achieved. In only a matter of seconds it doubled, then tripled my top speed, and soon the boat was disappearing again into the mist with hardly a wake trailing behind it. With a laugh I gave the crew a friendly wave as they vanished, knowing that we had been soundly beaten.

"We've gotta get us one of those!" I laughed as David caught up. "We'd be at the ocean by now!"

We continued on, and soon encountered another scull crewed by eight girls, but that one was going south. Its dark shadow rushed by in the fog, which had finally begun to lighten a bit as the sun grew in strength. Several minutes later another went by, this time crewed by young guys who looked to be around my age.

"We must be caught in a parade!" David chuckled. "Where are all these things coming from?"

We reached Lake Beresford as the last remnants of fog vanished, and at its mouth was assembled a practical fleet of watercraft: racing sculls, kayaks, and even a few canoes. Coaches were shouting orders from small motorboats weaving between them.

"They've gotta be part of a school or something," David observed.

We slowed for a few minutes to watch several sculls take off south in what was apparently a practice race, then continued on with vigor. We passed briefly through the southwest corner of Lake Beresford, then followed the River west past Anhinga Bay. From there the River turned back to the north, and after the Whitehair Bridge—which we stopped under for a quick lunch—civilization disappeared. We were entering a section of the River we called the Forever Stretch, which skirted the southeastern border of the Ocala National Forest on the west and the Lake Woodruff National Wildlife Refuge on the east—a good thirteen miles of unbroken wilderness.

It was the middle of the day. The sun was directly above, making it useless to look for shade by skirting the banks. My shirt eventually became soaked through with sweat, so I took it off and laid it on the bow to dry. The marshes and prairies of the south were no more; up here there were true forests, dense and vast. Shaggy palms, furrowed pines, glowering oaks, stately cypresses, bushy ashes, towering water hickories, and many others I couldn't identify were all entangled together to form a living wall rising on both sides of us, their boughs glinting and rippling in the breeze.

Our pace was fine, and yet as an hour, then two hours passed by, we seemed to be going nowhere. Every turn of a bend yielded the same view, and after a while it started to fool with my mind. The impression of going in circles, or of those dreams where you travel on and on but never get anywhere, steadily grew in my mind. The logical part of me of course dismissed it as ridiculous, but the feeling nevertheless started gnawing away at my will. It was exactly why we had called this run the Forever Stretch.

David began taking more frequent water breaks, so many that it eventually started to affect our progress. He picked up the pace for a bit when I mentioned it, but then slowed again. Several times I paddled for a good five or ten minutes without thinking, then looked back to see him far in the distance.

"I need some food," he said shortly as he caught back up after one of these incidents.

I was getting a little frustrated. When we had been traveling at a good pace it still felt like we were going nowhere, but with these frequent stops our progress seemed torturously slow. Every minute we had to stop was a minute lost. I sighed and quickly scanned the area. "Looks like there's some high ground under that big oak up ahead. Let's stop there and take a five-minute break. Sound good?" David nodded silently, his face hard.

We pulled up the kayaks under the shade of the forest canopy, opened up our food bags, and quickly dug in. A breeze played gently through the boughs above us, scattering the light in dancing figures upon the damp earth at our feet.

"It's my shoulder," David finally said. "I thought that after being okay yesterday the pain might go away again, but it's getting bad."

"When did it start bothering you?"

He nodded south. "Before we reached Lake Beresford."

"Why didn't you tell me, man?"

"I thought it would go away," he repeated. "I was hoping it would...but I don't think that's gonna happen this time."

I was silent for a little while, then, "You think you can make it to the Astor Bridge?"

"I'm gonna have to!" David gave a weak laugh and looked around at the encompassing wilderness. "There's no help out here!"

We set out once more. I tried to slow my pace a bit, but David was really starting to drag. It wasn't long before he was taking more time to rest than he was paddling.

"We've gotta pick up the pace a bit," I called, looking up nervously at the falling afternoon sun. "At this rate we may not even get to the Astor Bridge before nightfall." I waited briefly for David to catch up. He looked bad.

"My shoulder's killing me, buddy," he apologized. "Every time I take a stroke it's like knives stabbing me."

I took another quick glance at the sun. "Okay, I'm gonna slow down just a bit more and you see if you can stay up with me. As long as we can just keep moving we should be alright. The fastest way to get you out of that boat is to keep paddling."

David nodded. His face grew red with pain as he strained to match my speed—he wouldn't be able to go much farther in the shape he was in. I can't even tell you how long we went on like that, limping down the River as the sun sank farther and farther from its noonday roost. I kept waiting, hoping for the next bend to reveal some kind of civilization, but every turn gave way to more impenetrable forest. How could we not have reached it by now? Could we have taken a wrong turn somehow? No, no, I knew that was impossible—there were no other major rivers here.

"Can you believe this?" I said out loud, "It's like we're—David?"

I looked back to see David drifting up behind me. What had been crimson red on his face was now a pale, sickly white. Beads of sweat were pouring down from his forehead even though the temperature had dropped significantly.

"Sorry," he said, finally catching up, "I had to throw up back there."

I laid my paddle down on the gunwale as I looked at his face—this was getting serious. "Do you need to camp here tonight? We could maybe find a patch of dry ground and stay out in the—"

"No way," David replied flatly. "We can't be more than a few miles away from the Astor Bridge. Let's keep going."

"But are you okay?"

"No, but I'm certainly not going to stop here when we're that close to a road. Let's go." David set his jaw and began straining forward again.

Finally, I could see a larger body of water up ahead which I guessed was Lake Dexter, but I noticed something else, too. All this time, the thickly wooded eastern shore had been serving as a windbreak, but as it fell away up ahead I saw waves on the water.

"Looks rough up here!" I shouted as I felt the wind already growing. "Careful to—"

Suddenly, out of nowhere, the water several yards to my right began to churn with a roar. It was an alligator, a big one, racing toward me at full speed just below the surface of the water; the thrashing of its powerful tail was sucking the water down in a miniature vortex. Before I could even react it was upon me. For one sickening moment the swirling dark water rushed up, and I felt the banging of scaly ridges just under my feet. Then, just as the water was about to pour over the gunwales, I popped back up, and everything was instantly normal again. The whole thing had happened so quickly that the adrenaline didn't wash over me until a few seconds later.

"Whoa! Did you see that thing?" David called from behind me.

"Did I *see* it?" I yelled, "I practically did a belly flop onto it!" My fingers and toes were now tingling from the shock and my heart was pounding, but I quickly composed myself, thanking God for yet another rescue. "We've gotta keep moving, come on!"

A blast of fierce wind hit us from the northeast as we skirted the exposed western shore of Lake Dexter. The force was much worse than I feared, throwing us about in the open waters and trying to push us back the way we came. I heard David straining as we fought back with all our strength, making slow forward progress in the quickening chaos. Soon all other sound was swallowed up by the roaring wind, so we pressed on in silence.

Just to traverse the short distance of the lake took a great deal of time and effort. As we found the River again, I spied two crowded boat docks stretching out from the western shore ahead of us, seeming out of place amidst the otherwise unbroken wilderness. A channel marker stood defiantly against the waves in the open water about thirty yards ahead, and I aimed for it. The wind was now so strong that the entire surface of the water was surging back toward the south, taking on an appearance like whitewater. It had to be at least twenty miles per hour sustained, with gusts closer to thirty.

I reached the marker and grabbed it tightly, exhausted, but then I looked back to see David vomiting over the side of his kayak some distance away. The wind was taking him backward—he wasn't going to make it. Making up my mind quickly, I let go of my hold and was instantly swept back, reaching him in mere seconds in the seething torrent.

"Come on, buddy!" I shouted over the roar. "Just get to that channel marker up there and we'll tie the boats to it."

David barely even looked up, his face miserable. He managed a slight nod and grit his teeth as he struck the water once more. The distance that had taken me seconds to cover heading south now took nearly ten grueling minutes fighting north, but we finally made it back to the marker and tied off. The rushing water gurgled against the underside of the boats as they held fast.

David collapsed into his seat, his clammy face twisted with pain and his eyes closed tightly. He laid like that for several minutes, not moving at all. I was almost about to check if he had passed out when he finally opened his eyes and looked over at me.

"I can't do it, man."

"What do you mean?" I asked, surprised by the finality in his voice.

"I can't make it any farther."

"Yeah you can; I know you can. The Astor Bridge is only a couple more miles away."

"I can't fight this wind," he shook his head weakly. "My shoulder's completely gone; I can feel bone grinding against bone every time I move it. I can't make it."

"I'm not just going to leave you here...what are we gonna do?"

David motioned west to the boat docks nestled among the thrashing trees.

"We don't even know where that is!" I protested. "How could we even have someone come to get you? Our best bet is to get to the Astor Bridge."

"Daniel," David looked me straight in the eye, "I'm telling you right now I can't make it. You know I wouldn't say that unless there was absolutely no way I could go on. I'm in the worst pain of my life right now. I've got to stop." The desperation in his voice quelled any remaining arguments I had left, and I finally nodded.

"Do you want to wait a few minutes here?"

"No, let's just get there now."

I pulled the rope loose from the channel marker and once again we were swept south. Fortunately, traveling to the west was not quite as bad as going north, and within several minutes we had reached an old concrete boat ramp sloping up the shore on the north side of the docks. I stood shakily as my feet met land for the first time in hours, then helped David up. From the top of the ramp we could see RVs, fifth-wheels, and pop-up campers scattered about on green grass under the shade of towering live oaks—obviously some kind of campground.

"This has got to be it for me buddy," David said quietly. "I'm sorry."

"Don't beat yourself up," I replied quickly, "it's nothing you can help." But even as David trudged off to try and contact Jay, my heart skipped a beat as the implications suddenly hit me like a ton of bricks: if I was going to continue, I would have to go alone. It was what I had feared from the beginning but never let myself seriously think about until now. In an instant, I was overwhelmed by the vast distance still ahead of me, all the unknowns and uncertainties. I sat silently, deep in conflicting thoughts as I gazed out at the grey, wind-swept waters.

After a while David returned. "Okay," he said, "Jay is on his way out; he thinks he's got our location figured out. Did you want to swap boats?"

"No," I replied, still dazed, "I took Old Orange on my very first long-distance trip, and all these years she's been good to me. It only seems right that I should take her the rest of the way."

"I'll help you get whatever you need out of my boat, then. We'll rearrange it so it all fits in yours, then you can take off."

"What?"

"Yeah man, as soon as you're loaded up, get out of here; I've already slowed you down enough today."

"There's no way I'm just going to leave you. Jay may not be able to find this place, and you'd be stuck out here."

"I'll be fine, man! You should leave while you've still got enough daylight."

"I'm staying," I insisted. "I'm not going to decide my next step until I see Jay pull up."

We transferred the tent from David's kayak to mine. I grabbed the rest of his granola bars, crackers, and tuna packs to add to my partially depleted stores, and tossed him his sleeping bag out of Old Orange. But even as we were reorganizing I felt like I was just feigning resolve; the whole time I was almost outside of myself, like I was in a dream. Was I really going to do this alone?

We had no idea how long it would take Jay to show up. Once we finished the work, there was nothing to do but wait, and my growing sense of dread became almost suffocating in the idleness. My stomach knotted as my mind raced through everything that could happen if I set out alone. My very life could be on the line. But what would happen if I chose not to go—would I ever get another chance like this? The decision to back out now would surely haunt me.

We sat in terrible silence for a long time until I suddenly noticed movement out on the dock closest to us. Two old men were sitting in lawn chairs on the open, porch-like bow of an old houseboat, engaged in what looked to be fairly casual conversation. Without a moment's hesitation, I jumped at the opportunity to do anything besides brooding over my fears.

"I'm gonna go see if those guys can give me any advice on Lake George," I told David. "Be back in a minute or two."

I walked the short distance of a gentle grassy slope, then stepped out over the water on the wooden planks. As I made my way down towards them, the two men looked up and nodded. I tipped my hat to them.

"Good afternoon, sirs."

"You look like you've had quite a day, son!" said the one on the left, a tall man with a large, weathered nose and a thin facade of grey hair. "Where'd you come from?"

"Well, today we started about twenty-five or thirty miles south of here, but we've been traveling for five days now. We started in Blue Cypress Lake, about..." I took a moment to do the math, "...I guess about a hundred and sixty miles south of here."

"A hundred and sixty!" the man repeated for clarity, then nodded over toward the boat ramp. "In them kayaks we saw you pull up in?" I nodded. The man spit over the side of the boat in disbelief and let a couple expletives fly. "How much farther you got, son? You ain't gonna cross George, are ya?"

"Well, that's why I thought I would come over," I explained. "I was planning on crossing it tomorrow, but I've never been this far north on the River before. I was wondering if either of you knew Lake George very well."

The man chuckled. "Son, I've lived 'round here nearly my whole life. I've traveled George in just about every size and every kind of boat you could think of."

"A kayak?" I asked, raising my eyebrow.

He stopped short. "Well, not a kayak. I'm talking about motorboats. Ain't no way I'd take something like that across that lake!"

I cringed. "It's that bad?"

"Oh yeah," he replied without hesitation. "Those waters can get like the ocean, especially in squalls like this," he nodded at the seething River beyond. Even though we were sheltered by the thick forest just north of us, the howling wind could still be heard. "I've been sunk out there in boats this size," he pounded the deck of his boat a couple of times with his shoe. "When that lake gets angry, you don't want to be anywhere near it."

I gulped, and my voice cracked a little as I managed to reply, "Well...I have to try."

"Where you tryin' to get to anyway, son?" the other man finally spoke. He was much shorter, with smaller facial features and dark eyes hidden under bushy grey eyebrows. He sported a worn fishing hat, with wisps of wild white hair poking out from underneath it.

"Well, me and my buddy over there were trying to break the speed record for kayaking the entire St. Johns River...so we're planning on reaching the Atlantic."

The big-nosed man whistled, then laughed, "I didn't even know you could get to the ocean from here!"

"But my friend hurt his shoulder pretty bad," I continued, "so I'm wondering if I should...well...it looks like I'm going to have to go alone. Do you think there's any way I could make it across Lake George in that kayak?"

"Not with wind like this!" the big-nosed man replied. "You'd get sunk in no time! There'll be big ol' swells with white caps out there right now—and that's what gets you, the white caps. When those big waves start breakin', they just dump right into your boat. Why, you'd probably go down under just one of the waves that are cookin' out there right now!"

"It's not usually this windy up here, is it?" I asked, hoping that perhaps this was just an unusual day. But the big-nosed man shook his head.

"Naw, this is pretty normal for up here."

I thought for a minute. "Do either of you know what tomorrow is going to look like? I've got to cross that lake one way or another."

"Tell you what, son," the other man said, "I'm fixin' to head over to my boat anyway. Come on over there in about five minutes, and we'll take a listen on my NOAA radio and see what the conditions should look like tomorrow."

"That'd be great! Which one is your boat?"

"You can't miss it; it's the run-down piece-a-trash that looks like an old shed on pontoons, over that way," he pointed over to the second dock.

"I'll be there. Thank you!"

As I headed back, I was surprised to see Jay's truck backing up to the kayaks. He jumped out.

"So, shoulder trouble, eh?"

"Yeah," David replied dejectedly, "it's totally gone."

For a moment Jay looked like he would say something light-hearted to soften the blow, but as he looked at David's face he caught himself, gave a slow, understanding nod, and laid a hand on his back. "I'm sorry, son."

David swallowed hard, staring blankly at the ground for a few moments, then took in a deep breath. "Well, let's get this over with."

With hardly any gear left, New Blue was now pretty light, and the three of us maneuvered her into the bed with ease. We secured her down in silence.

"Well, what are you thinking, Daniel?" Jay finally asked. "You wanna hitch a ride with us back home...or are you gonna keep going?"

The old man's grave report of Lake George combined with the offer of a trip home was agonizing. I could just tell everyone that the conditions were too bad—it was a reasonable excuse. I hesitated, but then remembered the invitation to the other house boat.

"There's a guy over there who's gonna listen to the weather report for tomorrow. If you don't mind waiting a minute, I want to hear that before I make the final call."

"Go ahead, we'll wait for you!"

This time I walked down the second dock. I passed several boats bobbing around in their slips until, just as the man had explained it, a particular boat stood out like a sore thumb. It was literally a shed on pontoons! Despite my predicament, I couldn't help chuckling at the sight.

"Come on in!" I heard the man's voice call from inside as I approached.

I carefully stepped out, transitioning from the sturdy dock to the shifting deck of the boathouse, then fumbled through the open doorway. In the dim light of a single yellow bulb fastened to the ceiling, I could make out a neatly made twin-size bed in the far corner to my left, taking up nearly a quarter of the entire square footage. The man was sitting on the end of it, hunched forward toward the wooden shelving which ran across the full length of the wall to my right. A Welsh terrier slept at his feet.

The man looked up. "Have a seat, son," he motioned behind me, and I looked back to see a weathered white lawn chair up against the right corner. I took him up on the offer. It was only then, when I sat down, that above the creaking of boats and the distant howling of the wind I heard the small voice of a radio, and realized it was sitting on one of the shelves right by the man's head. He was listening intently, so I stayed quiet until he spoke first.

As my eyes adjusted to the light, I saw that every wall of the little house was covered with pictures. Some were very old black-and-white photos, grainy and yellowed in places, but a handful of them seemed pretty new. I saw giant mountain ranges, exotic beaches, friends with seventies-style hair laughing together on a lime green couch, young men in freshly waxed fifties cars. I noticed a formal one of a young man wearing a military uniform, and as I inspected it closer realized that it was the old man. No doubt about it, this guy had done some living!

The man finally straightened up, looked over at me, and shook his head. "Doesn't sound good, son—it's not supposed to be any better tomorrow. Wind might die down a little the next day; you could wait until then and give it a try."

"I can't do that," I replied quickly. "If I get delayed for an entire day, there's no way I'll make it to the ocean in time. I've got to cross it tomorrow or not at all. Isn't there any safe way to cross?"

The man thought for a few moments, the stubble on his chin sounding like sandpaper as he scratched it. "Well, at night that wind might die down a bit; if you tried crossing tonight you might find some calmer waters. Only problem is there's no lights out there and the moon won't rise 'til early morning, so you wouldn't be able to see a thing."

"Suppose I left at 4:30 or something like that. I could start in the dark for the first half and finish the second half with the morning light. Would that work?"

"I can't promise you anything, son. I'll be honest with ya, judgin' by what it's like out there right now, I'd say you'd have to be crazy to try to cross that thing in a kayak. I've seen a lot of boats get sunk out there—this ain't no game."

"But say I *was* crazy," I pressed, "and I *was* going to try to cross it, what would you say to do? What would be the easiest way to cross?"

The man looked me straight in the eye. "Ain't no easy way to cross George, son, remember that. Best advice I can give you—besides don't do it—is to get a good sleep tonight and wake up as early as you can. When you hit the mouth of that lake, you point your bow north and don't stop. You fly for that far shore like your life depended on it...'cause it might."

I walked back in the late afternoon light with my gut churning. The old man's report had been just about as bad as it could have been. It would be absolute stupidity to continue alone...I would have to call it quits. Jay and David saw me from a distance and were watching as I approached. I looked over just in time to see a great blue heron pumping its steel blue wings and landing softly by the water's edge. It puffed its feathers and cocked its head at me, as if waiting to see what would happen next.

"I'm staying." I was surprised to hear the words come out of my own mouth, firm and confident.

"You sure?" Jay asked. "What you guys have already done is amazing; no one would think any less of you."

No, I wasn't sure...was I? The greater part of me still balked at the prospect of facing the danger alone, but there was another part, small but quickly growing in strength, that wanted to jump and shout with excitement at the challenge. In what seemed to me like an eternity, but was probably only a moment, that small part gained the mastery.

"I'm sure," I replied. "I have to do this...for myself."

David smiled with approval and slapped me into a big bear hug. "You stay alive, buddy! Seriously, I'm so sorry I couldn't—"

"I told you, you don't need to be sorry. This isn't your fault. Don't beat yourself up about this."

Jay hugged me as well. "Take care of yourself, Daniel," he smiled, "and Godspeed!"

Afraid to let myself linger, I gave Old Orange a shove into the shallows and climbed in. I tipped my hat to the two of them as they stood by the truck, and with my heart pounding madly in my chest began paddling away. My speed, my progress, my success now rested solely upon my own skill and endurance. There would be no one else to account for or to blame—if the journey failed, it would be because I failed.

I was afraid, terribly afraid. I feared all the unknowns which laid heavy on every mile ahead. I was staking my life on this trip, now; if something happened to me out there, it could be days before anyone knew about it. I had never felt so small and vulnerable in my whole life, yet there was a strange sense of destiny in it all, as if the way everything was working out was exactly how it was supposed to be. I didn't look back, paddling with all my strength, gaining speed as I approached the open River once again, nervously singing the words of the old hymn,

> *When through the deep waters I call you to go,*
> *The rivers of sorrow shall not overflow,*
> *For I will be with you, your troubles to bless,*
> *And sanctify to you the deepest distress.*

The roaring wind burst over me in an instant as I cleared the trees, but without flinching I pressed my way northward against its fury. Jay and David disappeared, the boat docks soon after, and I was once more engulfed by wilderness. I didn't slow for a moment—I only had a couple hours of good daylight left. Our original campsite was now too far to reach in time, but the Astor Bridge, about two miles south of it, was possible. I would have just enough light left to reach the bridge and hopefully find a spot to set up camp for the night.

The wind continued unabated, funneling through the channel. It rushed across my ears so that all I heard was its howl for nearly two hours. The temperature was steadily dropping, and I could tell it was going to be a cold night. As the shores darkened and the blue sky dimmed, I began to fear I wouldn't make it, but finally after a long, exhausting battle, I turned the last bend and the Astor Bridge came into view. The wooded shores gave way to houses and boat docks, and just before the bridge itself were two marinas on opposite sides of the River. Marinas were typically kind and welcoming to travelers; they would certainly be my best bet at getting a place to pitch the tent.

"Alright," I prayed quietly, "there are two marinas, one on each side...which one should I choose?"

The one on the right.

As I paddled over, I noticed that the building seemed to be more of a restaurant. Its neon beer signs scattered pink and blue on the dark River, and the thick, greasy smell of french fries whipping by me in the wind reminded my stomach that it was well past dinner time. A wooden deck, upon which several people were talking and laughing around tables, stuck out over the water about five feet above the surface. A small flight of stairs led down from the deck to a handful of boat slips which were all full.

I made my way around the northernmost slip, squeezing my way through a narrow opening to one of the cleats along the side. I fished out my small length of rope, tied off Old Orange, and stepped carefully out onto the wooden planks. As I made my way up the stairs to the deck, several people fell silent and stared; only under their gaze did I suddenly realize I hadn't showered since the beginning of the trip. I smiled awkwardly, tipping my hat as I made my way through the door and into the restaurant.

The ice-cold air nearly knocked me backward as I stepped in, but I quickly recovered. The place was packed, obviously a popular spot in the area. Occupied tables and booths were all organized in an orbit around a bar positioned in the middle of the large room. I was quickly glancing through the windows behind me at the dying sun when, above all the buzz of countless conversations around me, I heard the most unlikely exclamation.

"Daniel Robison! I don't believe it!"

I spun around, wondering who on earth would have any idea who I was. I scanned the crowd and suddenly identified a smiling face looking over at me. It was...Country!

Here I have to pause and give a little background for this encounter, or else it just won't seem as incredible as it really was. Country was the nickname of one of the guys who worked with my fiancée, Nicole, at the University of North Florida in Jacksonville. A month or two beforehand, I had mentioned the St. Johns trip that I had been planning.

"No way!" he had said, "I'm gonna be out on the River that same time!"

It turned out that UNF had put together a team of students and professors to take a trip through several sections of the St. Johns River for a variety of learning opportunities, ranging from history to the ecology of the River itself. They would be traveling by boat through much of the middle basin.

"Maybe we'll meet up sometime," he had suggested jokingly, both of us understanding the vast area we would be covering. The chances of us meeting at the right place at the right time completely by accident would be close to impossible, and consequently I hadn't given the conversation a second thought since...yet now here he was! If I would have come any sooner, any later, reached our original campsite, or gone to the marina on the west bank, I would have passed him by without ever knowing it.

Country quickly got out of his seat and maneuvered around a couple of tables to reach me, then shook my hand and slapped me on the shoulder. "I can't believe it!" he repeated, shaking his head. "Never in a million years did I think we'd actually bump into each other out here!"

"It's great to see you, Country!" I laughed in astonishment. And I meant it. After everything that had happened that day, it was truly a comfort to see a familiar face. He motioned for me to follow him back over to his table, where a group of about fifteen sat over their meals.

"Guys," Country announced as we approached, "this is Daniel Robison; this is the guy I was telling you about!"

One of the girls threw down her napkin. "Are you serious? You're the guy that's kayaking the whole St. Johns?" I nodded sheepishly, causing the whole table to erupt in oohs and ahs.

"What's the distance you've covered so far?" another woman asked—I couldn't tell if she was a younger professor or an older student.

"Something like...uh...well, somewhere between one hundred and sixty and one hundred and seventy miles." Again, oohs and ahs ensued.

"Country kept telling us about you while we've been out on the water," an older grey-haired man smiled. "We were wondering if we would see you sometime!"

"Weren't there two of you, though?" asked one of the guys in the back.

"There were two of us, but my partner injured his shoulder and had to drop out a few miles south of here."

"So you're going on alone?" a professor asked with concern.

"Yeah...it's just me now."

"Are you crossing George tomorrow?" The question caught my attention, and I looked over at the clean-shaven, middle-aged man in the salmon fishing shirt, sitting at the other end of the long table. Anyone who was on a strictly first-name basis with Lake George was not from Jacksonville—this man was a local.

"That's the plan for now, yes sir."

"Captain Dave," he introduced himself, leaning over the table to shake my hand. "Just call me Dave."

"Capt'n Dave's the one who's been taking us around everywhere," Country explained. Everyone at the table gave a little cheer, and the captain rolled his eyes and waved it off. Then he looked back at me.

"Have you ever been out there before?"

"Well, no," I admitted. "I just talked to some local guys a few hours ago, and they were telling me that it can get pretty rough out there."

"It can indeed," Dave nodded gravely. "I live just north of here, and I've seen it get nasty...especially with weather like this."

"They told me I should head out early in the morning and just make a straight shot for the far shore across open water...would you agree with that?"

Dave frowned. "I would agree with starting early; the wind'll die down at night. As far as the 'straight shot for the shore' bit, though, I don't think that's the best strategy for you. It'll take hours to cross, even at your max speed, and if you run into trouble you'll be far from safety."

"So you're saying I should take the long way around, along one of the coasts?"

"That's what I would say. Wind's going to be coming in hard from the northeast tomorrow just like it is today, so your best bet will be following the east coast. If you stay close enough, the forest'll block a lot of that wind for you."

Everyone had finished eating, and now began filing out the door to head back to their boat. I followed them out onto the deck, still talking with the captain. Once outside in the growing chill, the group huddled around me to say goodbye.

"Do you have anything warm for tomorrow morning?" the grey-haired professor spoke again. "It's supposed to get pretty cold in the early hours."

"No, I don't have anything warm except a beanie and a wool scarf somewhere in my dry bag. I guess I just wasn't expecting it to get cold in mid-March." Even as I spoke I suppressed a chill as I stood there in my sweaty old bathing suit and T-shirt.

"You could get in bad shape if you don't have something to keep you warm out there," Dave admonished.

"I've got a thick sweatshirt back on the big boat," Country told me. "It's anchored just a couple miles south of here. I could go in one of the small boats and get it, then bring it back over here for you to take."

"You can have this if it fits you," one of the girls offered, taking off the hoodie she had been wearing. It was a deep navy blue, and at the top right corner a twisted leaf had been embroidered—the insignia of the UNF Environmental Department.

"I don't want to take your hoodie!" I protested.

"You'll get much more use out of it than I will! We've got a couple extra on the boat anyway." She handed it to me and I tried it on. It fit perfectly! The lingering warmth on the inside made me realize just how cold I had been.

"Thank you so much; this will be a huge help!" I told her.

"How about a windbreaker?" Dave asked. "Do you have one of those?"

"I don't."

One of the professors quickly reached into a docked boat and pulled one out. As he brought it back into the light, I saw that it matched the hoodie. "Here you go," he said. "Please take it as our small contribution to your adventure."

I received my second gift with equal gratitude. "Thank you all for the help. I hope the rest of your trip goes smoothly as well."

"Remember to go up the east coast," Dave cautioned as everyone started piling into the two boats waiting for them. "You don't want to test that lake by going up through the middle. Just get up as early as you can and stay to the east."

"I will," I nodded. "Thanks a lot, Dave."

"If anything happens, or if you need anything at all," he handed me a small slip of paper, "my number's on there. Give me a call anytime, day or night, and I'll do whatever I can to help."

"That's great to hear, Dave; I really appreciate it."

He gave me one last handshake, then followed the others into one of the boats. Country slapped me on the back as he made his way on board.

"Safe travels, man! Hope you make it to the ocean!"

Everyone waved goodbye as the two boats started up, pulled away slowly, then headed back south in the fading light. I watched them as they grew small in the distance until all I could make out was the white wake stirring up behind them. My heart leaped as I suddenly realized I hadn't secured a place to camp yet; hopefully the owner would be friendly, or I would have to search for a place to sleep in the dark!

Fortunately the owner, Zach, was great. It took me a few minutes to convince him that I wasn't making up my story of how and why I got to his establishment, but once he saw that I was serious he told me to come around back and he would set me up. Immediately south of the restaurant was a narrow channel that led into a small, L-shaped harbor lined with boat slips, about half full. I paddled to the end of the north arm of the harbor, tied off, and met Zach at the giant live oak less than twenty yards from the water. The entire area under its sprawling boughs was clean grass—it was perfect. Zach even offered to help me unload my gear, and I was so tired at that point that I didn't refuse.

I had the tent set up and all of my things inside in just a matter of minutes, having become quite proficient at the process over the last several days. Twilight grey was yielding to a clear, starry night as I settled myself in. Zach stopped by once more to drop off a thick blanket just in case it got too cold. I was confident that my sleeping bag would be sufficient, but I thanked him and accepted the gift all the same. I ended up using it as an extra cushion underneath me, which made it the most comfortable night of the whole trip!

It was quiet by the oak tree. In that sheltered space, the rushing wind had been subdued to a gentle breeze that rippled against the tent like a lullaby. My little room now seemed enormous, almost empty with only me and my gear. It felt strange to be alone, but at that point I was still riding the adrenaline of it all. The one thing that loomed heavily on my mind, spoiling the otherwise beautiful night, was the knowledge that before dawn the next morning I would be attempting to cross the second largest lake in Florida in a small recreational kayak. I'm not ashamed to say that I felt the worst fear of my whole life that night. What if I got sunk? What if I couldn't get to shore? What if I died out there...would anyone even find me? No one was forcing me to do this, I was choosing to take the risk...was I doing the right thing? Had this ceased to become courage and degraded into recklessness?

I realized I had forgotten about Nicole's note for me the day before; I had been so tired that I had fallen asleep without even thinking about it. I searched through the sleeve of my journal until I found it.

I'm not sure where you are, but I'm sure it's beautiful. I know you're not losing steam yet, but here are some words of encouragement: "...be content with what you have, for God has said, 'I will never leave you nor forsake you.'" (Hebrews 13) I love knowing that God is with you every moment of this trip. I know he will protect you and provide a way for you.

I paused, then read aloud, "...for God has said, 'I will never leave you nor forsake you.'"

Vast choirs of crickets were well into their familiar strain now, and the proud canopy of the oak above rustled sleepily to the song in the tranquil night. I took in a deep breath, released it slowly, packed up my things, and finally crawled into my sleeping bag. With the pen from my journal, I slowly wrote out the words on my hand:

I WILL NEVER LEAVE YOU NOR FORSAKE YOU

THE NORTHERN FRONTIER

The alarm shrieked in the darkness—how could it be 4:00 already? A shiver ran down my spine as I forced myself awake and climbed out of the sleeping bag into the cold. With renewed gratitude I put on the hoodie that had been given to me by the UNF crew the night before, and also dug out my woolen beanie and scarf from the bottom of my dry bag, having never expected to actually need them. I had only a bathing suit for bottoms, and the only close-toed shoes I had were my big boots which had long been soaked through, sitting in the back of Old Orange. I would have to be content with only my top half warm.

Breakfast consisted of an energy bar, some dried fruit, and a pack of crackers, but I shoved some granola bars into my pockets for quick access later. I packed everything before finally unzipping the tent door, then hesitated as I looked out into the dark of a 4:30 morning. My muscles were stiff and I was drowsy, not to mention overwhelmingly anxious. For a second I almost convinced myself to lay back down and get a little more sleep, but then hardened my will, gritted my teeth, and stepped out into the chill with the gear in my hands.

As I approached Old Orange, I saw that she was completely covered with a thick blanket of dew from bow to stern, and I was careful not to brush my new hoodie against her as I loaded the dry bags. Barely more than five minutes later I brought the tent as well, then found a spare garbage bag to use as a seat cover between me and the dew. I looked over the black, glassy water of the little harbor. Everything was still now; even the crickets had been silenced by the cold night.

I glanced down to see the scripture written on my hand and smiled to myself. I would never feel ready, I just had to start...now. I hushed the hundreds of wild thoughts racing through my mind as I climbed into Old Orange, forcing everything in me to a calm stillness. I was completely resolved—there was absolutely no way I was turning back now. My boat would have to be sitting at the bottom of Lake George before I would give up. I had to try. My heart raced as I untied myself from shore and pushed off, slicing silently through the black. I worked up to a good pace within my first few strokes, and the long blades of my paddle seemed to move the stars as they dipped into reflected space.

Once I made my way back out into the main channel of the River, I found a ghost town. The thin row of darkened buildings were disfigured by dim dock lights, and eerie shadows played through the thin fog that swirled over the water. Even the restaurant, which had been so warm and welcoming the night before, now stood empty and lifeless as I passed under the Astor Bridge. Up ahead were a couple more old houses along the banks, but beyond them I couldn't see a thing—no water, no trees, no sky, just blackness as dark as pitch. I passed the houses quickly, and in the last pale glow from Astor I could just make out another bend up ahead. Fighting my better judgment, I rounded it and was immediately consumed in complete darkness.

There was a large splash somewhere on my right, and I remembered my encounter with the alligator the day before which had nearly sunk me. I tried to stay levelheaded in my blindness, but my nerves were on edge. I placed my paddle down quietly across the gunwale and pulled my dry bag into my lap, forcing myself to make every move deliberately and calmly. I fumbled around inside until my fingers closed on my small headlamp, and I fitted it on.

With a click, a small spot of the world reappeared ahead of me in a dull grey, illuminating the red fire of two alligator eyes which flashed for a moment, then disappeared beneath the surface. I breathed deep and looked around, trying to get my bearings; there appeared to be the dim shadow of another bend less than a quarter-mile ahead, so I aimed for that. Another heavy splash came from my left this time. I lit up the area in an instant, but there was nothing but silent ripples. There was a sudden thrash in the water to my immediate right, so close that I felt it through my paddle, and I started with a shout.

For a split second, the writing on my hand flashed in the beam as I took another paddle stroke. "I will never leave you nor forsake you," I recalled it aloud; "I will never leave you nor forsake you."

Instantly, my mind was back with Spencer and Joey on the very first canoe trip we had ever taken on the River many years ago. We had left in the dark of an early morning on the third day of that trip, but in the humid heat of summer rather than in the chill of spring. Out there on the dark River, we had been completely surrounded by a chaos of huge alligators splashing and slapping the sides of our boats, and we had been afraid for our lives. But we had started singing songs to God, and it had driven both our fear and the alligators away.

I gulped, then attempted to sing quietly—nothing came out but air. It was too early in the morning to have the option of volume; I would have to belt it out or stay silent. I hesitated for a minute or two, a little embarrassed to just start singing out loud even in that isolated place.

Suddenly to my right, there was a crash of underbrush followed by another heavy splash.

I started singing.

> *Shall we gather at the river,*
> *Where bright angel feet have trod;*
> *With its crystal tide forever*
> *Flowing by the throne of God*

I startled as the echo of my voice came back to me from the black forest, but I kept going.

> *Yes, we'll gather at the river*
> *The beautiful, the beautiful river;*
> *Gather with the saints at the river*
> *That flows by the throne of God*

I clicked off my headlamp. Very slowly, stars that had been invisible to me before began sparkling out as my eyes adjusted, until soon they were blazing brightly in the cold morning. I could hear a soft wind shuddering over the topmost boughs of the forest canopy. My heartbeat slowed to its normal pace, the terror melted away, and it was beautiful again. Once more my mind was at peace with the task at hand, and I continued on, still singing as I went.

> *Ere we reach the shining river,*
> *Lay we ev'ry burden down;*
> *Grace our spirits will deliver,*
> *And provide a robe and crown*

> *Yes, we'll gather at the river,*
> *The beautiful, the beautiful river;*

Somewhere along the way I must have passed the campsite we had originally intended for the previous night, but I don't know where; my entire trip to Lake George was completed before dawn. It was still dark when, rounding a bend, I caught sight of a single yellow light up ahead by the east bank. As I came closer, I noticed an old wooden house, standing mostly hidden in the thick shadows of the forest that surrounded it. It seemed incredibly out of place—a single, weathered island of humanity set against those many miles of wilderness.

The light was coming from the top of a wooden post jutting out of the water, and as I reached it I grabbed on and pulled out a granola bar. I had just peeled back the wrapper and was getting ready to take a bite when a gust of freezing wind from the north took my breath away. It was not the calm breeze that I had been feeling on and off all that morning, but a biting, unhindered wind—the kind that comes from open water. The strength of it blew away the trembling fog, and all at once I realized where I was. In the darkness, I could just make out where the black silhouettes of both banks suddenly fell away ahead of me, and beyond them was a vast expanse of nothingness—Lake George.

Another gust blasted the boat again, and I held the post tight to keep from being blown backward. I got the whole granola bar into my mouth with two giant bites and swapped my hoodie with the matching windbreaker, not wanting it to get wet in whatever conditions might await me. I took a deep breath, and decided not to leave time for my better judgment to start nagging. I began paddling again. The wind's power increased as I pushed forward as if to warn me off, but I didn't stop. Both shores swelled out into darkness in an instant, and I nervously began my crossing.

Rather than following the shore all the way around the southeast corner of the lake before finally heading north, I decided to cut the corner to shave off some distance. Confused waves rocked me as I left the security of land behind and headed into open water; they were good sized, but not breaking. To the east, I could make out a grey hint of the coming dawn, but it would still be a while before the sun actually came up. I looked again to the north—there were no lights, no distinguishing features...nothing. It seemed like an unreachable infinity of rolling waves churning out from the horizon itself.

Another gust pounded, shoving me back several feet like a leaf on the water. My fingers began to sting with the cold, and a shiver went down my spine, but I didn't stop paddling. The southern shore slowly sank away behind me, and the sounds of early morning birds and rustling trees were swallowed up as my whole world became the restless surface of Lake George.

The farther out I ventured, the worse the waves became. It grew so chaotic that waves began charging at each other from completely different directions, and I was getting caught in the middle of it, tossed and jerked in the mess as I fought to keep my heading. For all my striving, the eastern shore was still just a black line in the dim distance. I remembered the words of Captain Dave and the old man on the houseboat: the lake would be calmer at night, but once the sun came up it would become wild again. I had to reach that eastern shore before the sun rose. I breathed in deep and quieted my mind until it was clean of thoughts, sharp and clear. I was fully present in the spray and the icy wind. I stopped worrying about time and distance and banished the mental map that I kept running through over and over again. No excuses, no distractions.

I plowed forward with new strength, tearing through the tumbling mayhem and forcing Old Orange to hold as straight a course as she could. Wave after wave, gust after gust, I fought my way across the open water and its worsening conditions without rest for a solid hour until, finally, I drew near to the shore. A thick clutter of cattail and giant reed lined the shallows, obscuring the bottom half of the towering forest that rose up beyond. It's canopy thrashed and swayed, buffering the now howling wind to create a narrow pocket of calm in its shadow where I was now bobbing gently, my wind-whipped ears ringing in the sheltered silence.

Red streaks in the sky signaled the coming day, and in the fiery light I spied the shape of a long dock only about a mile north of where I was, stretching a good way out into the shallows from somewhere within the mass of waving trees. I had not stopped since I had entered the lake, but urged myself to reach it before taking a rest. The thin currents of wind that were managing to strain through were already pushing me back to the south; at the dock, I would have something to secure myself to.

Dense mats of eelgrass slowed me down as I struck out again, so I was forced to nudge Old Orange to the west to get into slightly deeper water. Some chop returned as soon as I eased away from the shelter of the wooded shore, but I stayed close enough to keep the conditions manageable. I watched as the sky melted gently into blue, and pure sunlight finally began filtering through the gaps in the trees. The rising temperature quickly made the windbreaker uncomfortable, but I didn't want to stop until I was safely tied off against that dock. It loomed larger and larger as I closed in, stretching out roughly sixty yards into the water and standing seven or eight feet above the surface atop thick wooden pylons. At its terminus the dock split north and south like a T, and both of these forks ended in what looked like covered gazebos. Now that I saw it up close, I guessed that it was very likely part of something more than a personal residence, but couldn't tell for sure because its origin was hidden by the dense forest.

I coasted through the first set of pylons and crossbeams and finally brought myself to a stop at the second set, tying off the bow securely. I ate an early lunch, moored between the brilliant greens and golds of the shore and the rolling blues of the endless lake, but I couldn't stay for long. The wind and waves would grow in strength as the day went on; the sooner I reached the northern shore, the better. For all the work I had put in already, I was not even halfway across—ahead was just a horizon of water. I set my sweaty windbreaker inside out behind me to dry, stowed my food bag, loosened the bow line, and left the dock behind, continuing north.

A short distance ahead I noticed that the coastline seemed to fall away out of sight, then reappear about two miles farther north. As I came closer, I realized that it formed a large cove that carved nearly a mile into the eastern shore before curving back around again. The water between me and the far side of the cove was fully exposed to the fury of the northeast wind, seething and churning under its power. I stopped briefly at the southern tip of the opening to think things through. Sticking to the shore and traveling along the inside of the cove to the other side would take a considerable amount of time, time that would not be easily bought back. On the other hand, it beat sinking. I squinted north at the windy torrent, then east to the calmer—but much farther—shore of the cove, then back to the north again. I would once more try the open water.

"Come on, ol' girl," I patted the gunwale of Old Orange, "let's shred 'em!"

I was up to full speed in a matter of moments. The sun broke over me, now completely unhindered by the retreating shoreline, and a few beads of sweat ran down my brow as I raced forward. The jostling chop quickly grew into true waves, manageable at first, but more and more violent as I closed in on the middle of the funneling blast. Above the roar of the wind I heard one of them break, and my heart jumped. I turned to see the whitecap collapse into the crest of a neighboring wave, demolishing them both into a swirling mass of foam. It had been just behind me. Another larger wave broke a little ways to my right, spraying against my arm. It was becoming dangerous fast, but there was no turning back now.

My muscles were tense as I made scrupulous changes in speed and direction with every stroke, carefully navigating my way through. I went moment by moment, interpreting the size and shape of each barreling wave as if it were the only one. That was all I could focus on; there was too much happening to see the big picture. One careless move could end everything. Finally, after what seemed like hours on full alert, I passed through the center and worst of the chaos, and the waves slowly began dying down. I successfully crossed the mouth of the cove and came back behind the shelter of the wooded eastern coast once more. I was still not halfway across the lake, but I was beginning to make out what I thought was the faint dark line of a shore on the far northern horizon.

From that point on the eastern shore held no more surprises, and I had but to follow it all the way up to where the River would reappear. It is much easier to write this, however, than it was to actually do it. Because of the eelgrass which I mentioned earlier, I continued to keep out in more open water, not far from the coast but far enough that I was not under the full shelter of the forest. Because of this, I had to battle against a constant northeast wind for the next seven miles.

I took breaks as little as I could manage, since every time I stopped I would be blown back several hundred yards. The force of the wind became so severe that I paddled almost exclusively on my left side to counteract the resistence. My muscles ached, and I pushed myself so relentlessly that I began to feel feverish. I lost all track of time, both my mind and body growing numb as my paddle strokes became mechanical; conscious thought ceased, and my whole reality became a half-awake, nauseous exhaustion. I have no idea how long I went on like that until I realized that the northern shoreline was growing ahead of me, taking on definition. Finally, after what seemed like an eternity, I was able to make out where the rolling waters of Lake George ended, funneling into a narrow band of dark blue etching its way through shuddering bands of golden reeds. The River!

As I slowed my paddling for the first time in hours, a heavy weariness washed over me and my head swam. I felt so weak; it was all I could do to gently guide Old Orange along as the waves, which for the whole morning had fought against me, now admitted their defeat and admirably changed course, pushing me the final small distance to the mouth of the St. Johns. I cleared the last clutter of reeds and found myself looking at a line of houses, boat slips, and marinas strung out along the bank. I picked a marina only about half a mile away and, not daring to stop until I had my feet firmly on land, headed for it with the little strength I had left. I sucked in air as I inched along, straining against my narrowing vision until I was close enough to make out the sign: *Georgetown Marina.*

I let myself drift the last hundred yards or so to a stretch of covered boat slips, found an open one near the end, and nudged up against the wooden walkway. I clumsily tied off Old Orange, heaved myself onto the weathered planks, and collapsed. I drifted in and out of consciousness, my senses muffled and dark. Space and time fell away, and I felt myself floating dumbly and aimlessly through deep shadows. The next thing I can remember was a voice suddenly piercing through the nothingness.

"Hey, you ok, son?"

Suddenly I became aware of the wooden deck under me, and the puddle of drool that my face was laying in. I remembered that I had eyes, and upon opening them was startled to see a world of golden light and radiant blue. Everything seemed jumbled at first, but slowly my mind began to wake. Sun, earth, water, air...my trip...the crossing. I carefully lifted my head to see two men and a woman, all of them easily in their seventies, sitting on an old wooden bench just a couple yards away. All three were staring at me with amused grins; I'm sure I looked quite a sight.

"Are you ok, son? one of the men asked again. "Where'd you come from."

"I...uh...came from the Astor Bridge Marina," I replied as loudly as I could manage. Apparently it was loud enough, because they all gasped.

The gentleman closest to me let out a loud laugh and slapped his knee. "Woowee!" he shouted, shaking his head and looking toward the other two, "He's been a ways, ain't he?"

I managed a smile, and slowly lifted myself on shaky legs. I grabbed one of the wooden pylons supporting the tin roof above me.

"Where you goin' to, young man?" the woman asked, taking a sip from the soda can in her hand.

"The ocean...I hope."

"The ocean? Well, you still got a long ways then, don't you?"

"Yes, ma'am," I nodded, looking out over the River behind me, "still a long way yet."

My head was foggy. I couldn't steady myself, and my whole body felt so weak. I couldn't keep going like this. I hauled up my food bag and water jug and staggered to the west side of the marina where there was a small grassy area. Collapsing under the shade of a large oak tree, I wearily dug out a second lunch. From that spot I could see the way I had come, Lake George sparkling beautifully.

"Hopefully I can take it easy the rest of the day," I said to myself as I chewed on a granola bar.

I rested for nearly an hour after lunch, just watching the clouds and the rustling leaves, and as my body began absorbing the food I felt my strength and wits slowly returning. I was still exhausted, but my mind was clearer now. Finally, I gathered up my things and headed back to Old Orange. It was hard climbing back in after an already challenging day, but I soon felt a second wind as I pulled away from the docks and back out into the River.

From Georgetown Marina, the River headed straight in a northwesterly direction for roughly two miles. The wind had died down and there was a very strong current pushing me along, so I covered the distance quickly and easily. I made such good progress, in fact, that I dared to hope that perhaps the rest of the day would go just as well. Perhaps the current would be like this the entire rest of the way to the ocean! At the end of those two miles, however, the River turned straight north, and as I rounded that bend all of my short-lived hopes instantly disappeared.

The wind, which had plagued my crossing of Lake George, had not vanished after all, but had merely been blocked because of the angle of the River. This new northern stretch funneled the gale with such force that the caps of the waves were being whipped off and scattered as a driving mist into the air. I drove the blades of my paddle deep into the churning water, slowly moving forward against the fury. The shoreline crawled by at an agonizingly slow pace, but I set my eyes forward and kept pushing, unwilling to relent. I fought my way up for nearly two more miles until the River took another change in direction back to the northwest.

I intended to round the inside of the coming bend, then make a straight shot back over to the far shore to shave off some mileage, but as I adjusted my heading the wind, which I thought could not possibly get any stronger, now burst against me with an even greater rage. I paddled furiously, but seemed to be in a stalemate. Since I couldn't go straight into the gale, I tried zigzagging back and forth. In most conditions, the progress I made would have been considered trivial, but at that point I was heartily welcoming any forward motion at all, and the tacking seemed to give me just the slightest advantage. I was barely hanging on, nearly all my strength spent, but I knew that the moment I stopped fighting I would be blown right back to where I started—that was the one thing that kept my aching muscles going.

Simply completing my intended maneuver around the bend, which under normal conditions would have taken only a matter of minutes, took me nearly an hour to complete, but I was finally able to return to the sheltered shore. The power of the wind was broken as I came back under the cover of the trees, and I dropped my paddle and fell back into my seat, breathing a sigh of relief. I took a few big gulps of water, then let myself drift down the River a bit until two fishermen came into view, lines cast expectantly from a small motorboat.

"Howdy!" I called over when I was close enough.

"A little windy out here for kayakin', ain't it?" one of the men asked, amused. "You headin' up much farther?"

"I've still got a good ways to go yet. Did you guys come from the north?"

"Yeah. It's pretty bad out on Little Lake George right now; I wouldn't cross it if I were you."

"Huh? What's Little Lake George?"

He nudged the tip of his rod upriver. "Just about a half mile 'round this bend here. It can get even worse than the big Lake George sometimes!"

I didn't remember seeing anything about a Little Lake George—maybe I had been so concerned with the big one that I had overlooked it. I hoped against hope that perhaps they didn't know what they were talking about, thanked them both, and continued on. Unfortunately, the two men had been much more informed than I had been. As I rounded the bend, the River curved back to a northerly heading and bulged out quickly, its width reaching about a mile and a half. The wind returned in all its fury, and there were wild waves out on the open water. Though I didn't stop paddling, my will hesitated for a moment. The waves ahead were the biggest and roughest I had ever seen in all my years on the River, bad enough to make me seriously question if I could make it through to the other side of the bulge, roughly two miles in the distance.

The waves quickly grew in size and power, and soon they were driving against me with their full force, empowered by the battle cry of the rushing, unchecked gale. My heart pounded as whitecaps appeared, some of them slamming against the sides of Old Orange and spraying me with icy water, but I didn't dare stop. I kept my eyes fixed on the far shore ahead and kept my bow pointed straight for it. The lake was slightly hourglass-shaped, so as I reached its middle the coasts pulled in closer and provided a meager windbreak for a short time, but all too soon they fell away again, and the waves grew worse than ever. A few of them managed to dump water into Old Orange, and it quickly formed a sloshing pool at my feet.

The whole crossing took roughly an hour and a half, and it was grueling work. I have always said that any ape with a paddle can use a kayak, but ninety percent of the strength you need for long-distance travel is not in your body, but in your mind and will. And there is nothing more detrimental, more sabotaging to your will than hindered progress. It chips away at your determination, leaves you feeling stretched and spent. That is exactly what I felt as I finally reached the northern shore safely.

A boat dock extended out from the shore but I passed it by, observing that it was a good ways into the afternoon now, and all the wind and waves of the day had slowed my progress significantly. I needed to reach the next campsite, Top Side Marina, which was still another five miles or so north. When I was planning the trip, I had only allotted twenty-five miles for that day, since I had no idea what crossing Lake George would be like. Ironically, Lake George had turned out to be the easiest part of the day, but I was certainly glad of the shorter distance. It would allow me to hopefully finish earlier than usual and get some extra rest.

After my battle with the unexpected Little Lake George, the River narrowed to only about three hundred yards. Though the wind continued to howl, there was no longer space enough for it to stir up big waves, and some of its force was stolen once more by the forests on the eastern shore. It made for a little easier paddling, which I was extremely thankful for.

The banks on both sides remained largely uninhabited and heavily wooded until the last mile or so, when I started seeing houses on the east side. They all sat high above the water, their properties held in by concrete or wooden seawalls. Many of them looked older but seemed to have aged gracefully, looking more like aesthetic compliments to the woods around them rather than competitors for space. Their appearance had the comforting, not-in-a-hurry feel which is common for many river houses, and I smiled as my thoughts turned to Jay's house, where he and David and the rest of their family were surely getting ready for dinner about now.

As I turned the last bend, I was met with another stretch of houses, but curiously enough, no Top Side Marina. It had looked pretty large on the maps I had referenced, surely big enough for me to pick out on the shoreline, but I couldn't see it anywhere. I drifted down a little farther and there was still no sign of any marina, so I made my way to a nearby boathouse. I heard talking from within, and as I closed in a man and woman came out of the screen door and sat in some lawn chairs on the deck.

"Hi!" I called over, waving one of my paddle blades their direction.

"Hi yourself!" the man smiled behind a pair of sunglasses. "Good day to be out on the water, huh?"

I nodded politely. Freak windstorms weren't exactly the kind of conditions I would have picked, but I supposed just about any day was a good day to be out on the water. I coasted up close to the deck. "I'm trying to get to Top Side Marina. It was supposed to be right around here, but I can't seem to find it. Do you have any idea where it is?"

He was a larger man—his stained T-shirt failed to completely cover a conspicuous beer belly which slumped a little over his belt. He was clean-shaven besides a peppered mustache that twitched as he thought for a moment. "That name doesn't ring any bells for me," he finally replied, "but I don't actually live here. I've just been helpin' my buddy build that log house up there." He pointed behind him to the beautiful cabin sitting above a high seawall of upright timbers. "He's been around this area for a while, though; let me see if he knows it." He

114

got out of his chair and hollered through the screen door, "John! Hey John, you know where Top Side Marina is?" There was a muffled reply from inside, but I couldn't make it out. The man shook his head in response. "No, not me; there's a guy on a kayak out here who's trying to find it."

"A kayak?" This time I heard the other voice clearly, and footsteps sounded on the wooden planks within. Another man appeared, looking a little older and thinner than the first, with white hair and a matching shaggy beard. His skin was dark and weathered and he was dressed similarly to his friend, the design on his T-shirt long since faded. He smiled and nodded a greeting when he saw me. "Where are you tryin' to get to, now?"

"Top Side Marina," I repeated. "It was supposed to be somewhere right around here, but I can't seem to find it."

The man squinted down the deck, scratching his chin a few times. "Can't say that I recall that name. Well...wait a minute...there was a marina some time ago, just over there," he leaned out over the water and pointed about a half mile upriver—there was nothing there. "I know it had switched names from somethin' or other just before I moved here, but then it closed. That was years ago; nothin's been there ever since."

"Well that's no good," I sighed.

"You may want to just go back to where you put in at, friend," the larger man suggested. "Where'd you come from?"

"I put in nearly two hundred miles south of here—I can't go back."

Both men paused.

"Hold on, son," the white-haired man finally managed, "did you say...two *hundred* miles?"

"Yes, sir. I'm trying to break the speed record for traveling the whole St. Johns River. I put in at Blue Cypress Lake six days ago, and I'm on my way to the ocean."

The white-haired man squinted hard at me. "You messin' with me, kid?"

"No, sir."

He studied my face for another moment or two, then smiled. "Well then, if that's the case, you're welcome to stay here as long as you need to!"

I was surprised at the sudden invitation. "Are you...sure? I don't want to intrude or—"

"Sure, sure, it's no problem at all," the man waved my words away with his hand. "Some friends are comin' over for a get-together tonight, but we'll be down here at the boathouse; you can pitch your tent on the far side of the yard up there, and it should be quiet enough for ya. There's a little ramp on the other side of the boathouse." He started walking around to the north side. "Come on over here and we'll pull you up, buddy." I gratefully took his offer and met him at the old concrete ramp at the water's edge.

The man shook my hand as I staggered out onto land. "The name's John."

"Daniel."

"Pleased to meet you, Daniel."

The other man came up behind him and shook my hand also. "Just go ahead and call me Bubba," he smiled. "Do ya need any help with anything?"

"Oh no, you guys have done quite enough by just letting me stay here. I've only got a few things. Can I keep my boat down here?"

"Not a problem," John replied. "Just scoot it a little over to the side there. Nobody'll mess with it, you've got my word on that."

I grabbed my tent, sleeping bag, and my two dry bags, and followed Bubba around a small wooden fence, then up onto the deck of the boathouse. From there, we trudged up a well-worn dirt path to the yard, watching our footing on the tangled oak roots. As we finally reached the top, I was surprised at how high I was—it had to have been a good fifteen or twenty feet above the water. The late afternoon sun sparkled against the swirls and eddies of the River below, and the uninhabited western bank loomed dark and mysterious, its forest canopy swaying in the wind like waves. I set up the tent at the south end of the yard—it was perfect. Not only did I have a tremendous view of the water, but the nearby oak trees subdued the wind to a pleasant breeze, which I guessed would keep me cool throughout the night.

Bubba came back over some time later while I was looking over my maps. "Just wanted to let ya know that we're fixin' to eat. There's plenty to go around if you want some, so don't be shy!"

The invitation was given so sincerely that I decided to take him up on it, and followed him back down. Several more cars and trucks were now parked down by the boathouse, and there was much more commotion inside than there had been before. Bubba led me to the screen door and pushed it open. It was much bigger inside than I would have thought, skillfully constructed around a massive old oak tree that was actually growing up through the floor and roof of the eastern half which was over the shore. Even a circular bar had been built around the girth of its trunk. There were several card tables and mismatched chairs situated around the room, many of them occupied by new faces. Other people were already lined up on the far side of the wall, dishing out food from various bowls and pans, and my mouth watered as I took in the smells.

"Hey ya'll, this is the guy!" John announced as he got up out of his seat and shook my hand once more, and everyone shouted a hello. "Now, we've got enough food here to feed an army, and we don't have near enough people to eat it all," John encouraged, motioning me toward the food line, "so you eat as much as you want."

Over dinner, everyone was eager to hear about my journey, and listened intently as I told the whole tale. They were particularly amazed at my gator tally, which at that point had reached a total of one thousand and twenty-one.

"Did you run into some big ones?" someone asked from the back.

I smiled. "I suppose it depends on what you call big, but we saw a bunch that were bigger than my kayak out there." Those who were close enough glanced out the north windows at Old Orange sitting on the bank and shook their heads in astonishment. "In fact," I added, "one of them almost sunk me yesterday just south of the Astor Bridge."

"So you just figured you'd get out here and paddle three hundred miles for fun?" a man asked in between bites of fried chicken.

"Well, it certainly hasn't been all fun," I admitted, "but it's something I've wanted to do for a long time; I just wanted to see if I had it in me to do it, ya know?"

"So how much farther do you have to go" a woman asked from a camping chair in the back.

"Should be about a hundred more miles, give or take a few."

"You think you're gonna make it?"

A man close to her rolled his eyes and set down his plate. "Jenn, why would the guy be out here if he didn't think he was gonna make it?"

"I *hope* I'm gonna make it," I corrected. "Every day has new challenges; all I can do is face each day humbly and do the best I can. I guess whether I make it or not is ultimately in God's hands."

"Well, here's to ya, Danny boy!" The man smiled, lifting his drink high, and everyone else followed. "May the River Rider find the ocean at last!"

After dinner, I decided to turn in for the night to catch up on some sleep. The sun was now sinking behind the trees, turning the sky to bursts of yellows and oranges. As I recorded the events of the day in my journal, I watched it stain crimson, then violet, and finally melt into a dark, starlit sky that quivered on the surface of the water below. The night quickly grew cold and I crawled into my sleeping bag, the tent walls flapping gently in the breeze as I packed up my things for bed.

I had done it. I had crossed Lake George and lived to tell the tale. I was now—at least from my perspective—in the northern frontier, unsure of what awaited me in the days to come. In the darkness, I could still make out the now faded writing on my hand: *I WILL NEVER LEAVE YOU NOR FORSAKE YOU*

"You didn't," I prayed as my eyes grew heavy. "You didn't let me down."

FACING THE TEMPEST

I had decided to wake up early again to get a good start before the daytime winds, but when I turned off the alarm at 4:30 I instantly fell back asleep. By the time I finally woke again, it was closer to 5:30, and the crescent moon had just crept above the eastern horizon, dimly casting its almond glow.

"It's alright," I muttered, "I'm sure I needed it. There's still a couple hours before sunup."

I ate a hurried breakfast and packed up my gear. For a moment I thought about knocking on the door of the cabin to thank John and Bubba for their kindness, but as I had no idea how late they had been up I decided against it. As I made my way down to the now deserted boathouse, I could still make out the sound of a radio which had been left on from the night before. Two men were busily talking on some kind of early morning show; besides their voices, everything else was still and quiet in the darkness.

I quickly loaded my gear, then gave Old Orange a good shove out into the water. I climbed in, and after giving the boathouse a ceremonial wave set my sights northward yet again. As on the previous day, I had bundled up to stay warm in the chill, but even though it was actually colder that morning it somehow felt more refreshing than uncomfortable. After a few minutes of paddling, all the tiredness was gone and I was back to my normal cruising speed.

From John's place, the River held a northerly heading for about six miles up through the Seven Sisters Islands. By the time I reached them, the sunrise was already fading into a blue morning sky and a moderate northeast wind was forming over the water. Still, the conditions were peaceful enough and I made the most of it, keeping a good pace. Once past the Seven Sisters, the River bent east for about four miles, passing Murphy Island and the opening of Dunns Creek. I kept to the sheltered shore and was able to stay within the calm provided by the woods there. While I couldn't actually feel the wind for more than an hour, I gradually began to hear it growing in power, whistling through the tops of the trees overhead.

Finally the River turned north again, and the shore that had been protecting me was exposed as I followed the bend. There were no serious waves, but the wind itself hit me like a brick wall; I was engulfed in its roar, and my first few leisurely hours of the day came to an abrupt end. The force was intimidating, but I was much more prepared for it now than I had been the day before. I pressed through, slowly but steadily making my way up the channel.

The short four-mile stretch took me nearly two hours to cross. I didn't stop for food or water until I reached a point where the River cut back sharply to the south, creating a small pocket of shelter. Nestled along that muddy shore were two long wooden docks stretching from either side of a concrete boat ramp. I tied up at the end of the closest dock and hopped out with my food bag for a quick break.

Looking at my map, I saw that the River cut south for barely half a mile before swinging back around to the north again like a big sideways S. After completing that maneuver, the Memorial Bridge should be directly ahead, and from that point on the River would begin to broaden considerably. In the upper basin where David and I had begun, some parts of the River had been narrow enough to almost straddle both banks, and in the middle basin its width ranged between roughly one to two hundred yards. Since Lake George, the River had widened to roughly a quarter mile in some places. After the Memorial Bridge, however, the River would soon bulge to a mile and a half across, and eventually swell to nearly three miles farther north. If the conditions were barely navigable as they were, what would be waiting for me beyond the bridge?

A grim foreboding began to churn in the pit of my stomach, but I fought against it. "I don't know for sure," I mumbled. "Let's just wait and see."

I had no problem covering the short half mile of the switchback under the shelter of the bank. As I followed the bend around to the north again, a tall arched bridge appeared—the Memorial Bridge, just where it was supposed to be. Just south of the bridge, several men were talking and laughing along an old wooden dock with fishing poles cast. Watching them in the light of that beautiful, clear day, I dared to think that perhaps I had been worried over nothing; maybe the hardest part of my day really was behind me. But that pleasant thought only lasted for about a minute.

As I drew closer to the bridge and got a clear view through its pylons, a chaotic, tempestuous scene awaited me. True to the maps, the River almost instantly swelled to take on the appearance of a small lake, angry and formidable. The laughter of the men, now sounding more like a taunt, quickly died away as furious gusts of wind funneled at me, warning me to turn back. I came under the shadow of the bridge, and suddenly the navigable waters were transformed into the biggest waves I had seen yet.

They were jumbled, having no order or predictable movement, and I was barely able to keep myself from being smashed against the nearest pylon as I struggled for any kind of control. One wave broke just to my right and dumped several gallons of water into Old Orange, drenching my side. Another followed over the bow, dropping another gallon or two. My balance started to falter as the extra weight sloshed around in the bottom, and as I looked out over the windswept northern stretch before me I could see nothing but an endless battle of white water, crashing and seething in the merciless wind. And just like that, without any warning, my will broke. Before I was even out from under the shadow of that bridge, I turned around and fought myself back toward the shore.

I took on another gallon or so of the River before I finally reached safer waters once more, trembling. My heart pounded as I looked back at the tempest. There was no way, absolutely no way I could get through that. With wind and waves that powerful, I would be swimming within a half mile of passing the bridge, I was sure of it. After six and a half days and over two hundred miles, I was beaten. I would get a hold of Jay and tell him that it was simply too much; no one could blame me for—

"No," I heard myself say aloud. "This can't be the end."

I struggled within myself as if I were divided in two, prudence and risk battling with one another as I drifted silently by the shore. Then I looked down at my hand. The words I had written two days ago were barely visible anymore, but the scripture had been burned into my mind: *I WILL NEVER LEAVE YOU NOR FORSAKE YOU.* If I waited any longer, fear would get the better of me and I would talk myself out of it. If I was going, it was now or never.

I charged. Gritting my teeth I met the chaos again, but this time I didn't slow down. The spray of the thrashing waves had me soaked within moments. I cleared the bridge and now met, not only the waves, but the wind in full force. Never in all my planning of that trip had I even remotely anticipated coming face to face with such raw power. I was no longer being merely tossed, but *thrown* from one wave to another, as if the near three hundred pounds of myself, my gear, and Old Orange were a paper toy. Still I fought forward with determination, my jaw clenched through the cold spray and the roaring gale.

I honestly have no idea how I did it, but after nearly an hour-long battle I finally covered the mile across open water to the safety of the eastern shore. Just as suddenly as the tempest had appeared, it vanished as I again came under the shelter of the trees. I collapsed back into my seat and let out a long, exhausted sigh of relief, feeling as if I had been holding my breath during the whole crossing. But my fight wasn't over yet. The wind was so powerful that even though it could not reach me directly, it was creating a reverse current over the surface of the entire River, forcing it to surge south. I realized that I was getting sucked back fast and returned to action, digging in my paddle to beat the opposing flow. I couldn't stop. My progress was slow, but gradually I was able to work my way up the east bank.

I fought north for two and a half miles before I ran into another dilemma. From its northerly heading, the River now cut straight east. I knew from looking at the maps earlier that after roughly three miles it would turn back up to the northeast, then after another four and a half miles turn straight north again. Keeping to the eastern shore would add extra mileage, and with the kind of conditions I had been encountering, where a mile could take an hour to cover, it was simply out of the question. The problem was that to cut to the inside bank, I was going to need to cross nearly a mile and a half of open water once again—water that seemed to be getting worse by the minute. If I could reach it, I would be sheltered for the three miles of the eastward stretch.

I decided not to hesitate—things were not likely to get better by waiting. I broke away as my shore made its turn to the east and met the gale again in its full fury, getting thrown and smashed as before. As I feared, it had indeed grown worse. Many of the angry white crests of the waves were rising to eye level with me now, and despite my best efforts to maneuver through them I began to take on water. Several times I found myself caught in the trough of two waves that were barreling toward one another and feared that I would be sunk, but each time I miraculously escaped the pounding collisions. After nearly an hour I reached the shelter of the far shore, but couldn't stop because the River was still surging backward.

There were many houses along the shore here, and almost all had a dock in one form or another; some looked like glorified wreckage, while others stood upon towering concrete pylons which seemed to proudly defy the hectic current racing around them. I weaved in and out of the structures as I went until, after another hour, I saw where the River made its turn back up to the northeast. Before I reached the bend, however, I sensed that something was wrong.

I could physically feel tremors in the air from the wind battering through the channel ahead. The water was different than I had ever seen it—not the deep, lazy blue that I was used to, but instead a kind of electric cerulean, slashed into ragged, swirling shapes by the white froth rushing across its surface. There was something eerie in its movements as it seethed out from around the bend, something hostile and violent. I can't explain it, but the colors, the sounds, even the smell in the air seemed to strike at some primal part of me, and a panicked fear leapt inside. The feeling was so strong that it made my stomach churn, and I let myself slip back several yards to the last dock before the open water.

I tied off to one of the wooden pylons, and the swift current quickly yanked the rope taught as it swept by. I took my first gulps of water since before the Memorial Bridge and, finding that it helped with the nausea, decided to try eating something, too. I took my time, munching on peanuts and granola for nearly fifteen minutes until I felt strength slowly returning...but it never fully returned. The temperature had not risen above the low 60's that day and I was starting to shake, still soaking wet from my two earlier battles. But there was nothing I could do for the moment; if I was to change clothes, they would just get drenched again. I sealed up my food bag, took a deep breath, and untied myself from the dock.

As I approached the turn of the bend and the torrent beyond, terror welled up in me again. I felt a surge of anger, then bitterness, then a tear fell from my eye as a wave of sadness hit me. The sensation was bizarre; it was as if my own body was trying to override my resolve and force me to back down, that's the only way I know how to describe it. But I kept going. I cleared the actual shoreline, and now only a thick mess of thrashing reeds shielded me. The gusts began finding their way through and popping my ears; white froth was bubbling through the dense golden stalks like the mouth of a rabid dog. All my deepest instincts recoiled at the raw power that roared ahead, but my resolve held out.

I cleared the reeds, and before I could even turn my bow north the blast caught me broadside and plowed me south with the River. I recovered quickly, digging my paddle in on one side and orienting myself dead into the barrage. It was unbelievable. There were no more gusts; the wind now drove full force and unabated. I don't have words to describe the incredible power that I suddenly found myself confronting; every obstacle before seemed like child's play in the face of such relentless force. It took me nearly ten minutes just to fight my way back to where I had started by the reeds, then I pushed northward. Waves began to appear as the shore gradually fell away, leaving me completely unguarded. They started small but grew quickly, and within several minutes had grown to dangerous strength and assumed one unified direction: straight for me.

Now, you should never go straight into a wave. If you do, the sleekness of your bow works against you, cutting into the wave instead of rising over it, and consequently bringing the crest to break right into your boat. The safest way to get over them is to take a roughly two or ten o'clock angle. But I quickly realized that if I turned Old Orange any direction but twelve o'clock, the wind would overpower me and sweep me sideways. There was no other way forward but to push dead ahead.

The giant waves swelled, their crests mangled with angry white foam ready to crash, and I fought to keep Old Orange afloat. The only thing that kept me from sinking straight into the waves was the distance between them. If the troughs had been only a little smaller, I would not have been able to adjust the pitch of my bow in time and would have been sucked under. When I say I had just barely enough room, I mean it; the bow plunged underwater every time I reached the bottom of a trough, and each time I would fight back up to the surface just before it reached the gunwales. My entire front end would be thrown upwards into the air as I raced up and over the crest, my stomach would lurch with the momentary freefall, then I would plummet down the other side to repeat it all over again.

All my senses were on high alert; my speed, angle, the distribution of my weight all had to be perfect on every single wave to keep me above water. One wrong move and I would be sunk. The worst part of it all was that the western shore, about a hundred yards to my left, was barely crawling by. It would have been one thing if I was fighting for my life and actually getting somewhere, but my forward progress seemed to be happening in mere inches. I didn't stop, though, and neither did the windy tempest. Our strengths clashed amidst the froth and spray, creating a near stalemate but for my meager advancement. The wind refused to let up for me, and I refused to surrender to its maddening claws.

I worked hard to silence my mind from worrying about time and distance, and focused solely on the precision adjustments to make it up and over each wave. Finally, after hours of that grueling battle, I could see ahead where the River turned north once more. I knew that somewhere several miles ahead on that east bank was my endpoint for the day, but I was on the opposite shore. I would once again need to venture across.

I had become more or less indifferent to being soaked at that point in the day; the icy spray that constantly stung against my hands and face no longer got a flinch out of me. Several inches of water sloshed around in the bottom of Old Orange from a few very near misses, but I had quickly figured out how to compensate for the constantly shifting weight—there was no stopping to bail it out. Nevertheless, there was definitely a coldness that was setting in, in the very core of my body. It was a deep cold, a bone cold, not yet severe but steadily growing. I did my best to push it out of my mind.

I was coming close to the end of the northeastern stretch, and could now see all too clearly two miles of the roughest water yet between me and the far east bank, stained a sickly, angry green by its unrest. I could hear some of the riotous crashings of the fierce waves even above the roaring wind.

"How can I cross that?" I whispered breathlessly. "I'm barely staying afloat as it is!"

I suddenly noticed movement to my left—a man and a boy were standing at the end of a dock, only about thirty yards to my left. They were watching me.

"No harm in taking a little detour before the crossing," I suggested to myself, eager for a reason to postpone the agony, and carefully adjusted my course ever so slightly. I brought myself up to within a few yards of the dock, but couldn't stop paddling even there. Had I tied off to one of the supports, my bow wouldn't have had enough give to ride over the waves, which were still large even so close to shore. I grabbed my water bottle and risked a swig between strokes.

"Howdy!" I called over to the man and the boy, who were now leaning at the railing.

"Did you get caught in this," the man shouted, "or are you actually out here 'cause you wanna be?"

"I wanna be!" I replied, laughing at my own answer.

"Cool!" the boy smiled. "Where are you going?"

"To the ocean!" I smiled back, and watched the amazement in his face grow. "I'm trying to travel the whole St. Johns River; I've already gone about two hundred and thirty miles or so!"

"Two hundred and thirty...*miles*?" the man repeated for clarity.

I nodded. "My campsite's somewhere over on the eastern shore, so I've got to cross that open water. I'm not gonna lie, I'm pretty nervous about it!" I looked up at the sky. "I'm running out of daylight fast...do you think I'd be able to make it to the other side before the sun went down?"

"Friend," the man laughed, "if you've been out all day with conditions like this, there's no doubt in my mind that you can cross it." The boy nodded encouragingly, obviously hoping to watch.

"Well," I took one more quick gulp of water and began edging away, "I'd better get to it, then! Thanks for the conversation; it's been a while since I've talked to somebody!"

"Sure thing! Safe travels!"

"Safe travels!" I heard the boy echo just as his voice was swallowed up in the gale.

When I thanked the man for the conversation, I had really meant it. I was amazed at how simply seeing and talking with another human being had lifted my spirits. I felt reenergized. So, man and boy, if by some chance you ever stumble across this—I suppose you'll know I'm talking about you—thank you!

I transitioned into open water, and as expected I was pounded like never before. An extra gallon of water was sloshing around in Old Orange soon enough, and I was getting worried. The waves were much rougher, and their movements harder to predict than they were closer to the west bank. But I couldn't turn back—the kid was still watching! I set my sights toward the dark line of the eastern shore in the distance and plowed forward with all the strength I had left.

It was late afternoon; the sun's scattered rays on the chaotic surface of the water were not quite so blinding now, more of a mellow gold. I still had time, but not much. Within two hours or so twilight would be setting in, followed by a quick nightfall with no big city lights to delay it. The deep cold inside of me was uncomfortable enough now that I could no longer ignore it. I began to feel strangely sleepy but pushed through it—there was no other choice in the middle of the tempest. I was able to maneuver and paddle but my mind seemed dull, only half awake. The cold slowly worked its way from my core out to my extremities, and my arms grew heavy.

Somehow I managed to make the far shore close to McCullough Creek. The wind, which had pounded my ears for so long, vanished immediately as I once more came under shelter, but my head kept throbbing with its pulse in the silence. I would have been more excited at having completed the final crossing of the day, but by that time my body was shaking hard and I was utterly spent from the fight. After spending a full day soaking wet in the cold, I could tell that something in me wasn't right. The sun was hanging low on the horizon, and I had only a precious hour or so before night was upon me. I was alone, exhausted, and running out of time.

I had two campsite options which had been found for me by Jimmy Orth, the executive director of the St. Johns Riverkeeper. Jimmy had graciously searched his database for Riverkeeper members who had homes on the water, and I had been assured that they would be on the lookout for me. Eli's place was roughly eight miles north of where I was, but Dan and Jenny's place was only about three miles. Of course, I wanted to shave off as much mileage as possible from the coming day, which could—I thought with a cringe—be just as bad if not worse than today. But I had never been more exhausted in my life; was it really worth completely wearing myself out just to get a few miles farther? I chose the closer.

I only took a few minutes to rest—I could do all I wanted of that once I finished for the day. From that point on there were many houses with docks extending far out into the water, and I made a distracting game for myself by weaving in and out of their supports as I sped by, now unhindered by wind or wave. The sky began slowly cleansing itself to a colorless white, preparing for sunset.

I had a description of the dock, and after about three uneventful miles I began to look for it: a long wooden dock with a green aluminum roof at the end of it. The sun was just touching the horizon when I saw it. Was I just seeing things, or were there people out on it? It *was* people! I could see them waving as I got closer, and my eyes welled up with tears as relief washed over me.

"Hi Daniel!" a woman's voice shouted.

I couldn't tell which of the three dark figures she was, but I waved back all the same. "Howdy! I'm guessing you guys are Dan and Jenny?" Even as I called out I was coming up fast, now only about fifty yards away.

The figures watched me close in until I was almost directly below them by the supports of the dock. In the dying light, I saw that the woman was in her forties with sharp features and a dark brown ponytail resting on one shoulder, dressed simply in a t-shirt and jeans. The man next to her was comparable in age and dress, clean shaven with peppered hair that hung just over his ears. Behind the two stood an older man in a polo and shorts who was grinning wide and taking pictures as I stared up at them.

"Come on over to the boat ramp on the side of the house," the younger of the two men directed me cordially. Against the bright pink of the sky, his hand pointed up the darkening shore to where I could just make it out. Beyond that, a large but clearly older two-story house with worn wooden paneling stood proudly in the middle of the property under the weak glow of a few exterior lights. My small welcoming party followed me down the dock and met me at the shore, and the younger man helped to pull Old Orange up onto land. He put out his hand as I climbed out.

"The name's Dan."

"Daniel," I replied, giving it as firm a shake as I could manage.

The woman came up and shook my hand as well. "Wonderful to meet you, Daniel! I'm Jenny. And this..." she looked over her shoulder at the older man and he stepped up, still smiling wide.

"Eli," he introduced himself, pumping my hand. "My house was the other one that was open to you. I knew this was the night you were supposed to be coming through, so I figured I'd come by Dan and Jenny's place to make sure I'd be able to meet you either way!"

"Thank you so much for opening up your homes to me! Do you know each other pretty well?"

"We actually just met Eli about fifteen minutes ago when he showed up at our door!" Jenny laughed. I jumped as a black mass suddenly darted across the yard and down to where we stood at the water's edge, big enough to be a lion. "Oh, and this is Coby..." she introduced the giant dog, but there was an air of concern in her voice. "Dan...uh, do you want to get him?"

"Hold on a minute," Dan reassured her, "let's just see..."

Everyone paused in silence as Coby approached me cautiously, looking suspicious. I slowly stretched out my hand and held it there, letting him come to me. His nose closed in and gave a quick, wet nudge, then another. Finally he relaxed and licked it, then came in close for me to pet him.

"Huh, look at that!" Jenny remarked. "Coby usually isn't fond of strangers; he's still pretty suspicious of Eli!"

"Maybe it's the smell," I laughed. "I'm sure I probably smell a lot more like a dog than a human right now!"

"Well, I'm heading back home," Eli announced, shaking my hand once more. "My wife cooked you up a nice hot meal and wanted to make sure it got to you. Dan and Jenny already have it sitting in the kitchen. Didn't know how picky you are, but I hope you like it!"

A hot meal! My legs nearly buckled at the thought. "I'm very grateful to you, Eli. Please tell your wife thank you for me. I hope she didn't go through too much trouble—"

"Nonsense! Any friend of the River is a friend of ours. It was our pleasure!" He reached into his pocket and handed me a small business card. "I'm sure you're itching to unload your things and rest, but my number and email address are both on here. When you finish your trip, I'd love to hear from you."

"Absolutely!" I almost put the card into my pocket, but then remembered it was soaked.

"It was a pleasure meeting you, Daniel," Eli smiled. "Safe travels!" And with that he disappeared around the side of the house.

"You look pretty cold," Dan observed, and I realized that I was visibly shaking as I stood there dripping. "You'd better take a hot shower and get your core temperature back up."

I froze. Up until that moment, I had sincerely forgotten that showers existed. Just the thought of hot running water was such a pleasure that my head began swimming. Coby watched in amusement as I hurriedly set up the tent and fished out some dry clothes with teeth chattering, then followed as I headed into the house through a sliding glass door.

Jenny greeted me there and led me through the large bedroom I had entered into, which I guessed was the master. As we walked out of the room, I was surprised to find no large open space but rather a narrow hall. A set of spiral stairs led up to the second story on my immediate right, and the front door was straight ahead. On either side of the front door were other doors. The whole layout of the house seemed to be stringently compartmentalized. Where was the kitchen and the living room? I followed Jenny through one of the doors which opened to a smaller bedroom, and at the far end was a bathroom. A towel, soap, and shampoo had already been laid out by the sink.

"I think you're good to go," Jenny said, "unless you can think of something else you'll need."

"Oh no, I'm fine. Thanks so much, Jenny!"

I had been trying hard to hide my shaking, but once she closed the door I let myself go. It was an effort to grip my wet clothes securely enough to strip them off, but I was finally able to accomplish the task. I reached into the shower and started the water running, but as I stepped back I caught movement out of the corner of my eye. I spun around to face it, heart racing, and saw a naked, sun-darkened man sporting an unkempt beard running up into a tuft of disheveled, dirty hair. My fear quickly turned to confusion, then melted into laughter as I realized it was a mirror!

Now, I don't typically use very hot water in the shower, but I did that day. It was exactly what I needed. In mere minutes it seemed to wash away not only the sweat, grease, and dirt, but also all the toil of the day. By the time I stepped out, my exhaustion had lifted, my head was clear, and I felt like my normal self again. I went back out the way I had come, now donning a black bathing suit and the first T-shirt I had laid my hands on in the dry bag. I climbed the staircase to the second floor, and was shocked to find it winding up into the middle of a large open area.

To my left there were a few couches and chairs positioned around a TV, behind which were large glass windows revealing a view of the dark River. To my right was an open kitchen, complete with a bar table that wrapped around the guardrail bordering the opening for the stairs. It seemed to me like Dan and Jenny's house was upside down—all their open area was upstairs and all the bedrooms downstairs. I had never seen a house with a layout like it.

"Feel better?" Jenny asked. She was chopping up some cucumbers next to a big salad bowl.

"Much better." I ruffled my damp hair as I reached the top of the stairs and joined her in the kitchen. Coby was lying by her feet, and pricked his ears up eagerly as I approached.

Jenny went over to a large paper bag. "This is the dinner Eli brought you," she said. "Didn't think to look inside it yet, but it smells amazing!" She opened it up in front of me and started pulling everything out. She was right, it *did* smell amazing! "You're welcome to eat some of the pasta Dan and I are having if you're still hungry after all this. Go ahead and start! I'm sure you're hungry, and this salad is gonna take a minute."

I didn't want to be rude, but my stomach was twisting with hunger after that long day, so I went ahead. The largest container was filled with steaming chicken and yellow rice, and surrounding the main course was a bowl of green beans and ham hock, seasoned red potatoes, several large hunks of freshly-baked cornbread, and oatmeal raisin cookies. After days of dried food from my bag, the tastes and smells completely overwhelmed my senses, and I had to keep reminding myself to breathe as I shoveled it down ravenously. Soon Dan appeared from somewhere downstairs, Jenny brought the salad and pasta out, and the two joined me.

"I love you, Dan!" a voice squawked as Dan dumped a pile of salad into his bowl, and I spun around. A huge scarlet macaw was resting on a perch in a birdcage so large I couldn't believe I had missed it until then.

"I love you, too!" Dan called over his shoulder, then rolled his eyes as he grinned at me. "Don't mind her. She tries to suck up to me every time she sees something on my plate that she wants. So how has your trip been so far? It's been pretty windy out there."

"That's a fact!" I exclaimed. "I've never fought wind and waves like I fought today. Really, it's been a serious fight since about halfway through my fifth day."

"That's when your friend had to back out, right?" Jenny chimed in. "We heard that he got injured or something?"

"Rotator cuff," I explained between mouthfuls of cornbread, trying hard not to spew any crumbs. "He went as far as he possibly could, but in the end this wind got the best of him; every stroke of his paddle was killing him. He got a ride home from a small campground just several miles south of Lake George."

"You must have been pretty lonely these past few days," Dan commented.

I thought for a minute. "Lonely? I don't know if I would say I've been lonely. It's funny, but I really haven't done much thinking over the last few days. My mind has had to be so focused on each moment tackling these bad conditions that I haven't had enough time to be lonely, if that makes sense. But I definitely wish he could have finished this with me; we've been on a lot of trips together."

"Were you afraid to go on alone?" Jenny wondered. "I would be!"

"I was more afraid than I think I've ever been in my life," I confessed, gnawing off some meat from a ham hock, "but I just felt like I had to. I don't know if I'll ever get the chance to do this again—I had to try."

The parrot squeezed an "I love you, Dan!" into the conversation, but got no reply.

"Well, you've made it this far!" Dan congratulated me. "What's stood out to you the most on your trip?"

At first, I tried to select a certain event to talk about, but no response seemed to quite fit the question. It wasn't really a particular event that stood out to me most.

"I'd have to say...well, I guess it's the change that's been happening in me." What had until then been merely raw impressions and vague emotions began to take form even as I spoke the words. "It just seems like so often we have this impression that we've conquered nature. We push buttons and pull levers and imagine that we've tamed the world, but having this experience has made me wonder if in reality we've really just tamed ourselves.

"We distance ourselves more and more from the world around us, making ourselves more and more fragile and dependent in our little bubbles of plastic, steel, and glass. In those bubbles, it's easy to think that we've conquered the world. But when we step out with nothing but our own ability and strength—when we take the gloves off, so to speak—we find a world that is still wild and formidable, a world that doesn't bow to us. It's been incredibly humbling to take this journey; I truly don't think I'll ever see this River, or myself, the same again after this is all said and done."

"That's exactly why I think you're gonna make it," Dan smiled encouragingly. "You recognize that you're just a guest here—we all are. If more people had that kind of humility and respect for the River, we'd be a lot better off."

I smiled at the compliment, and all of us laughed as yet another "I love you, Dan!" came threateningly from across the room.

"All right, all right already!" Dan finally gave in and threw a couple pieces of lettuce into the cage.

We talked for a bit more, but by that point I could feel my body wearing down now that my stomach was full. I knew that the next morning I would thank myself for turning in early, so I thanked Dan and Jenny once more, gave Coby a couple pats on the head, then walked back downstairs and out the sliding glass door to the tent.

The air was cold, around mid-50s, and a gentle breeze rustled in the small oaks on the neighboring property. With no lights to be seen from the far western shore, the black face of the River seemed vast in the moonless night. Sleepy ripples sloshed in the swaying grasses at the water's edge. The raging tempest had finally been hushed by the darkness, and I took in a deep breath of the wonderful calm. I zipped myself into the tent and struggled to keep my eyes open as I unrolled my sleeping bag.

I crawled in quickly, and had barely put my head down before I plunged into an exhausted sleep.

THE STORM

The dark River was difficult to navigate, and the pale moon exposed only scattered shapes and silhouettes of my surroundings—nothing good enough to orient myself. I headed one way, but it turned out to be a dead end in a mucky slough. I tried another way, but got the same result. I went in every direction I could, but every way seemed blocked. I was trapped. What if I never found my way out?

Suddenly, without warning, a cloud passed in front of the moon, and what little light there had been vanished into complete darkness. Then I became aware of sounds on the unseen shore beyond; it sounded like large animals pushing their way through the brush. They were everywhere. No...no, it wasn't the cracking of brush, it was different. The sound was almost like water itself, but coarse and rough, like thousands of little impacts...like...rain!

I jumped awake in my sleeping bag, still in the tent on Dan and Jenny's property. The pitter-patter of a light but determined shower was drumming just above my head, and in the glow of the dim porch light I could see the droplets spattering and running down the thin fabric wall. I nervously reached out my hand and felt it—soaked through.

"Aw, man!" I wiped my hand across my chest and reclined back on one arm, but as I did I noticed that the tarp floor was wet, too. In fact, there were puddles all along the edges of the tent where the walls met the floor. I reluctantly grabbed a handful of the bottom of my sleeping bag, which had been nestled up against one of the corners—also wet. The filling between my feet and the outer layer had so far kept it from soaking all the way through, but it was only a matter of time.

I checked the clock: almost 6:00 AM, time to get up anyway. I curled up in the middle of the tent where it was still dry and ate a big breakfast from the food bag, feeling weak and sore from the previous day. Once I had gotten all of my things packed and ready, I unzipped a small section of the door and looked out at the dark sky.

The swirling clouds above made it pretty obvious that the rain did not intend to stop any time soon. It had lulled into a drizzle for the moment, so I took the opportunity to haul the dry bags down to Old Orange, having to dump some rainwater—and river water from yesterday—out before I loaded them. It was depressing having to pack a wet sleeping bag and tent, knowing they would stand no chance of drying in their sealed bags, but there was nothing I could do about it. I would figure it out later.

I had just loaded everything when Jenny appeared at the sliding glass door. Coby squeezed through as she opened it and ran over excitedly to greet me in the rain.

"A little wet this morning, huh?" she smiled.

"Yeah, all my stuff is soaked."

"Oh no! How will you dry it when you finish today?"

I shrugged. "If I can make it, I should be staying at someone else's home tonight. Hopefully they've got a nice open spot where I can set the tent up, and there's enough daylight left to dry it! I'm not gonna worry about it now."

"Well, I'm getting ready to leave for work in just a little bit, but I made some cinnamon raisin bread last night and wanted to see if you'd like a piece."

I had already eaten, but homemade bread is something one should never pass up. Coby and I headed inside after her, and a shiver ran down my spine as the temperature transitioned from the chilly morning to the cozy warmth of the house. Dan was already upstairs reading the newspaper and eating breakfast when we came up.

"Hey! Sleep ok?"

"I love you, Dan!" the parrot chimed in quickly, greedily eyeing the eggs on his plate.

"I slept great," I replied, "until I woke up and found that my tent and sleeping bag were all wet."

"Man, that's a bummer!" Dan shook his head. "Has it rained earlier on your trip?"

"It almost did a couple times when we were much farther south, but this is the first time it's actually caught up with me. Doesn't look like it's planning on letting up anytime soon, either."

Dan glanced out the window and agreed. "You got a rain jacket or something?"

"I've got a windbreaker, but it's not waterproof. That's about the best I've got."

Dan pursed his lips and seemed to be thinking.

"Here ya go," Jenny handed me a giant hunk of bread in a napkin. It was hot in my hand, and the warm smell of cinnamon that rose from it was marvelous. By the time I had finished, she was grabbing her purse and keys. She kissed Dan and gave me a hug. "Safe travels!" she told me. "I'm so glad you were able to stop at our place; you're welcome back anytime."

"Thanks for having me! I really appreciate all you guys have done!"

Back outside, as I was pulling out a garbage bag to make a dry spot for my seat, I heard the sliding glass door open. Dan was walking down with a bright yellow rain jacket in his hand.

"Go ahead and take this," he urged.

"Oh no, I couldn't take your stuff, Dan!"

"Don't worry about it," he held it out to me. "This is my old one I used to wear to work and I've got a newer one now. By the time you got to us last night, you already had hypothermia setting in—that's nothing to play with. You need to stay as warm and dry as you possibly can out there. Take it."

I hesitated for a moment, then took him up on the offer, putting it on gratefully.

"I'm heading out," he told me. "Do you need help with anything before I go?"

"I'm all packed and ready to go, but thanks, thanks for everything, Dan."

He shook my hand. "My pleasure, Daniel. You be safe out there!" With that he made his way back inside once more, waving behind him just before he disappeared inside.

I heard a car start up and pull away from the front of the house, and then there was only the sound of the heavy dripping from the oaks nearby—the rain itself had briefly paused in the swollen sky. I eased out into the dark water, waved goodbye to Coby (who had his nose pressed up against the glass door in a slobbery grin), and headed north, the black forested shore ahead silhouetted against the stormy grey.

There was barely a trace of wind at all, but the air was cold and misty against my face, and after only a few minutes the rain began again. As Dan had accurately guessed, I was glad to have his rain jacket;

everything but my top half was instantly soaked. I wished for a pair of rain pants as well—all I was wearing below my torso was my black bathing suit—but I figured it was better to have half of me warm and dry than none of me!

I kept up my pace, trying not to pay too much attention to the storm. I was hoping that eventually the whole thing would blow over and the sun would find its way through, but as I continued on the conditions got worse. An icy wet wind began cutting through the already chilly air. It was not strong enough to create giant waves like the day before, but it added a good deal of resistance to my progress and gave my bare legs a good freezing. The rain went on, diminishing to a pestering drizzle, then growing to a roaring torrent, then cutting back to light sheets, then drizzling again.

Morning had come, but only in the form of a barely noticeable grey glow in a small section of the black sky. Beyond that, there was no change from when I had started out from Dan and Jenny's place over two hours earlier. Everything was dark and dismal. Even the River itself seemed troubled, tossing a restless, ashy foam upon the wind-blown chop that covered its surface.

Through the misty rain, I saw that up ahead my way deviated from its northerly heading and leaned to the northwest, and at the bend loomed the dark shape of Shands Bridge. I aimed for the outside of the bend, heading out into open water to cut the distance, but just then the clouds darkened, the northeast wind rose in fury, and another downpour commenced. The storm dropped a heavy pelting rain for a good while, then thinned and began driving in sideways, stinging on the wind. I greatly misjudged the distance of my maneuver, and it was nearly an hour before I had crossed the cold open waters to the safety of the shore, the bridge now just ahead of me. The rain grew heavy again, and with great relief I finally coasted under the cover of the arching concrete giant.

I shook my head back and forth a couple of times, flinging spirals of water, then took in my surroundings. By where I was near the shoreline, the bridge dipped from its high point out over the middle of the River and came almost to water level, providing about eight feet of clearance between me and its underside. The roar of passing cars above reverberated in the air and tingled through the water. Three men stood just out of the rain ahead of me, fruitlessly casting fishing lines into the troubled waves.

"A little wet for boating, ain't it?" one of the fishermen caught my attention as he waved my way.

"Well, I can't call it pleasant," I confessed, "but I could think of worse places to be!"

"Well said, son," one of the other men chuckled.

After a quick water break and an early lunch under the bridge, I bid the fishermen goodbye and wished them a good catch, then continued on under the unchanged sky. The rain had lessened a bit, but was still falling. I quickly left Shands Bridge behind and covered the next four miles of the northwest stretch. From there the River righted itself for a fourteen-mile climb directly northward, which would keep me occupied for the rest of the day. I paddled hard against the biting wind and the dark, relentless rain, taking little more than an occasional moment to swallow down some water.

Within the first few miles of the northward stretch, the eastern shore which I had been following fell away to form a large cove that spanned nearly six miles from rim to rim. I could not follow the line of the cove all the way around to the far end without adding many more miles onto my trip and losing a great deal of time, so I decided to cut straight across the mouth. To my relief I was able to cross in less than two hours with little difficulty, and from the northern tip of the cove I could see an enormous bridge in the gloom, stretching across the massive three-mile breadth of the River: the Buckman Bridge, the longest bridge on the entire St. Johns.

I tied off to a boat dock to grab a bite to eat, and assessed the conditions for my next open-water crossing to the Buckman. The rain had slowed to a thick drizzle for the last half hour, but was making up for it with a stronger and colder wind which was blowing the surface water back south. Nevertheless, for some reason there were no huge waves like the day before. I would have trouble fighting the sheer force of the icy gusts, but for the moment it looked like the River itself, though by no means smooth, would not give me too much trouble. I would be able to keep a decent pace.

I set out again within just a few minutes, anxious about wasting too much time resting with the unpredictable storm. As I ventured out into the open water toward the Buckman Bridge, the freezing wind made quite a fuss—as I had guessed—but was not overpowering. All it got out of me was an occasional shiver, since my legs were still exposed and dripping wet. I let myself be blown a little westward as I paddled, so that as I successfully made it to the bridge some time later I was closer to the far shore. I took a quick break in the shelter of its enormous pylons, but as I stared up at their dizzying height I noticed a new set of clouds rolling in from the northeast, menacingly black against the now spent grey overhead. It was going to be bad, and I needed to cover as much distance as possible before it hit. After taking a swig of water, I set out once more at full speed.

About three miles ahead my shore fell away to head northwest, with the far shore wrapping around in the same direction about two miles farther across open water—five miles total. Somewhere on that far shore ahead of me was my campsite. Despite the weather conditions I had made good time—it was only early afternoon! If I could keep up the same pace for the remaining distance, it would be the earliest I had ended a day yet. On a normal day, five miles would not have been a big deal, but the impending black clouds assured me that it was going to be hard earned.

The wind began gusting in powerful bursts, heralding the approaching storm, and with it the temperature dropped and the waves grew in size. The western shore offered me no protection from the northeastern squall, and as conditions deteriorated my progress slowed. Old Orange began pitching in the angry waves, the black clouds closed in, and pinpricks of cold rain struck my hands as I pushed forward.

As the heart of it swept out over the River, I could see the rushing opaque wall of a solid downpour. The sun's already diffused glow was blotted out, and the sky became as dark as night. I grew nauseous as Old Orange was heaved up and down with dreadful force. Everything felt like ice, and my legs were aching with cold. In between waves I quickly pulled out the garbage bag I had been sitting on, slipped my bottom half inside it, and tucked the opening securely under my rain jacket. Even with everything wet, I hoped that it would hold in some of my body heat and drive out the chill. I gripped my paddle just in time to plunge into the next driving wave.

The wall of rain finally came crashing down on me, and even the bellowing of the wind was swallowed up as it shattered the surface of the water. I lost almost all visibility in an instant, and had to orient myself by the direction of the waves. I pushed my way through the fury, gritting my teeth against the raging gale and the freezing froth. It did not let up for nearly half an hour, and even once the rain lessened all other conditions continued fiercely. Just a few hundred yards ahead was the bend to the northwest, and in the distance I could just make out the grey line of the far shore—my destination.

Without hesitation I charged out into the open water, and the waves grew in protest. I felt like a bull rider getting thrown and jerked in the fray, the storm striving madly to throw me. It took all my skill to battle through that seething minefield of crashing waves, but finally, just shy of an hour later, I passed through the worst of it and found myself nearing the far shore.

"Yeah, all right!" I called out, raising my paddle in triumph and then breathing a heavy sigh of relief. Because of my choice to cut a more or less straight line up that fourteen-mile northward climb rather than follow the eastern shore, I had made incredibly good time that day. Had I done the latter, the ride would have been less bumpy, but all the extra mileage would almost surely have taken me into the evening before I reached the campsite. As it was, I made it to the house by late afternoon, well before sunset.

Almost as if realizing it had been defeated, the rain, which had been falling in one degree or another for the entire day, suddenly stopped as I paddled up to the large old boathouse at the end of a long, weathered dock. A woman in a white blouse and denim shorts was walking down it from the shore, waving.

"Daniel?" she called out when she was close enough.

"That's me!"

The woman stopped directly above me with a warm smile. "I'm Lane. So glad you could come and stay with us for a night! Just head over to shore, and I'll get Matt to help you pull up your boat."

The concrete seawall, spattered in a colorful array of snails and algae, rose about five feet above the water and held in the large sloping yard above. As I closed in, I was surprised to see masses of barnacles and jagged white oyster beds just below the surface, but then remembered that by this far north the River had become brackish. A young man around my age—I assumed it was Matt—was there with Lane, watching as I carefully grabbed the dock above my head. I hauled myself up into the yard next to them, carrying one of my dry bags and tightly gripping the rope that was attached to the bow of Old Orange.

"Everything else oughta stay in there pretty snug," I assured him. "Let's go ahead and try to pull her up."

It was a little rough lifting the bow to rest on the corner of the dock and the seawall, but once we had managed that, the rest was simply a matter of giving the rope enough of a tug. The stern slid up out of the water as the two of us pulled, and a moment later Old Orange was resting safely on the soft grass.

I shook the young man's hand after the quick task, then grabbed the tent. "I'd better go ahead and set this up," I told them. "It got drenched last night from the rain, and I'm hoping I can get it dry before nightfall."

"I think you've got a good chance of it," Lane observed. "Looks like all that rain is finally passing us by. I've got a shower ready for you when you're done with that; just come on up to the house, okay?"

I set up camp under the shelter of a giant oak tree. Its ancient, arching limbs created a dense canopy against the swift-moving sky above. The ragged clouds were finally parting just enough to let a couple rays of the late afternoon sun escape, and I positioned the tent to take as much advantage of it as I could, using one of my last dry shirts to wipe down the inside. I hoped that between the golden light and the rippling breeze it would dry in time. As I finished, a chilling gust swept up from the water and I shivered, realizing that I was once again getting terribly cold. I grabbed both my food and my gear and started up the yard, trying hard to keep myself from shaking.

Matt had headed off into the small cottage which sat close to the water's edge, so I was alone in the quiet which had fallen in the storm's wake. As I walked, I took in the enormity of the property for the first time. The yard rose steeply, and I climbed perhaps fifteen or twenty feet by way of several stone steps which jutted organically out of the grass. At the top of the hill was an enormous house. The large back patio was crowded with dozens of beautiful potted plants, many of which were growing well beyond their homes and into the nearby grass. Plumbago blues, jatropha reds, bunches of deep green sage and spindly rosemary, neon purples of coneflowers, and countless other colors and shapes that were unfamiliar to me were all growing wildly together in a wonderful array. It didn't seem unkempt but free, like the place was working with nature instead of setting up against it.

I came in through French doors and found myself in a large but modestly furnished living room, with a dining area on my left and a bright, open kitchen beyond it. Lane was preparing something at one of the counters.

"Hi!" I called as I stepped in, not wanting to surprise her.

She quickly stopped what she was doing and gave me her full attention. A few proud streaks of silver sparkled in her otherwise dark ponytail as she moved from the bright kitchen lights and smiled again. "Ready for that shower, I'll bet!" she laughed.

I nodded, teeth chattering, and followed her through the kitchen into another room, then into a long hallway. We went several doors down and then through one on the right. That door led into a room, at the far end of which I could see the shower.

"Your house is huge!" I exclaimed, feeling quite at ease in her presence. "I'm afraid I won't be able to get back out to the kitchen when I'm finished!"

"It took me forever to find my way around this old house when we first moved here," she replied understandably, then nodded toward the open bathroom door. "Everything you need should already be set out for you; take as long as you need. If you get lost, just holler and I'll come find you!"

"Thanks!" I called after her as she left me to myself, then hurried to get the hot water running.

After several navigational errors, I finally found my way back out to the kitchen feeling clean, refreshed, and best of all, warm. Lane was still in the kitchen, though she had made significant progress on the vegetables she had been chopping. I noticed that the bay window above the sink had the same look as the back patio, potted plants stretching beyond their bounds with leaves and vines hanging by the faucet.

"I love all the plants here," I commented as I studied them. "It makes your house seem...well, almost alive."

She smiled. "I feel that way, too. I have such a love for growing things; that's why we wanted to live on the River. There are so many things you can learn out here."

"I've always been interested in learning about native plants," I confessed, and at that her face lit up.

"Really? Well then you should try this flower I just planted a little while ago." With childlike excitement she disappeared through the French doors, then returned with a few pink blossoms in her hand only slightly bigger than a half dollar. "Try one of these!" she encouraged.

Not wanting to offend my host, I hesitantly picked one up and nibbled on a couple of the petals. I raised my eyebrows in surprise at the refreshingly sweet taste, and gratefully took the rest from her.

"You can boil those in water and make some great tea, too," she informed me.

Lane graciously poured me a tall glass of orange juice and I sat while she continued working on dinner, talking about my trip so far. Eventually our conversation turned to the storm which had rolled in the night before.

"It's always hard to start the day dripping wet," I told her. "The whole day it's always in the back of my mind that I'm gonna have extra work to do when I get off the water. But I'm grateful that this is the only time that—oh no! I've only been thinking about drying out the tent and completely forgot about my sleeping bag!"

"Oh, that's no problem, just bring it up to the house. We'll throw it in the dryer, and by the time you're ready for bed it'll be ready to go. As a matter of fact, why don't you just bring all your dirty clothes and we'll give them a wash."

"Are you sure? I don't want to be any trouble."

"It's no trouble at all! Go ahead and grab whatever you want cleaned and I'll throw it in for you."

I did, and as my things were being washed I was able to take a good little bit to relax for the first time in over a week.

Lane's husband, John, came home just as the tattered sky began to blaze with the fire of sunset. He greeted me kindly and had many questions about my journey, finding particular interest in my gator tally, which, since my sixth day, was holding at one thousand and twenty-one.

"I can't imagine that many alligators in one place," he laughed, shaking his head.

"I wouldn't have either if I hadn't seen it with my own eyes! It was certainly intimidating, but up here there are different challenges."

"I'm sure, especially the last couple of days with this wind! So tomorrow's the big day, huh?"

I paused, not sure what he was talking about.

"The beach, I mean," John clarified. "You'll get to the beach tomorrow, right?"

I thought hard for a moment, and my heart jumped as I realized he was right! "I guess I've just been focusing so much on each day as it comes that it hadn't even clicked, but ya, I guess tomorrow is the big day as long as I can make it another thirty miles or so!"

"I think if you've made it all this way, you'll be able to handle it!" John encouraged.

"I hope so, but I try hard to face each day humble; you just never know what's around the next bend!"

As the windows grew dark with night the exhaustion of the day swept over me, and I found myself struggling to keep my eyes open. I thanked both John and Lane, wished them goodnight, and trudged back down the steep stone steps in the darkness. Under one arm I held my dry sleeping bag, and under the other a bundle of clean clothes.

I hesitantly touched the tent as I reached it—dry! I checked a couple more places around the seams and there was not a trace of moisture left; those last few hours of waning light had apparently been enough! Delighted, I zipped myself in and set my things in order. A cool, refreshing breeze was blowing up from the River now, rustling the fabric walls and rocking the sprawling limbs of the oak tree overhead so that its leaves sounded like gentle waves upon a sandy shore. Some clouds remained in the sky, but here and there through the mesh roof I could make out a few stars burning in the dark.

I found my map and inspected it in the dim light of my headlamp, confirming that I was indeed only five miles south of downtown Jacksonville. Once I passed through, there was only another twenty miles or so before the Atlantic. All told, it would be about a twenty-eight-mile day, but there would be an additional factor to consider. This far north, an incoming tide would override the River's northward-flowing current, so I would have to sync my day with its flow so that it would work with me.

Fortunately, Jay had looked up some tide charts of the area beforehand, and I had recorded the necessary days in my journal. Referencing these, I found that high tide would be at 8:30 AM. After this, the River would rush back out into the ocean and reach low tide by around 2:50 PM. That was my window of opportunity. If I could get through downtown Jacksonville by the time the tide began to ebb, Old Orange and I would be pulled out with it, allowing us to achieve enough speed to reach the coast by sometime in the early afternoon. To do that, however, I would need to wake up extra early and fight the incoming tide all the way through the city.

After I had scribbled down some notes from the day and set the alarm for 4:30 AM, I finally took out my letter from Nicole.

I know the end of your trip is on the horizon, and I hope you're feeling good. Be brave, as always, and HANG ON! You're almost there!

The final day—I couldn't believe it was upon me. All this time I had scarcely allowed myself to hope that I would actually make it to the end of my journey, let alone get there in record-breaking time. Yet there I was, just less than thirty miles from the beach.

"Not time to celebrate yet," I counseled myself as I quickly dozed off. "No telling what you'll meet tomorrow."

THE BEACH AT THE END OF THE WORLD

Everything was packed. The early morning was crisp and cold as I looked out over the black expanse of the River. Its far western shore was no longer wooded as it had been for countless miles before, but was now twinkling with the white and yellow lights of houses. I imagined the eastern shore where I was probably looked similar. The River was most populated here. I turned, nodded a farewell to the house on the hill, then carefully lowered myself down from the dock into Old Orange. I shivered as I made first contact with the cold seat, but knew the discomfort would quickly pass. I took the familiar grip on my paddle and pushed myself away from the crusty seawall.

There was no depth or detail ahead of me in those early morning hours, so I relied on the passing eastern shore immediately on my right to guide me. It was lined with elegant river mansions now, with lights that pierced through silhouettes of towering trees and quivered on the water. I wove my way through the many docks until eventually I found myself making a turn around a large bend, and as the shoreline retreated the Fuller Warren Bridge appeared nearly two miles to the north, bathed in yellow light against the night. The shore continued falling away east, so I ventured out into the quiet open waters, keeping the bridge directly ahead. It was a dreamlike scene with the approaching city lights sprinkled like stars, and not a sound but the rhythmic gurgling of my paddle strokes.

I made good time in reaching the bridge, squinting against the brilliant lights as I made my way through its pylons. The two shores returned from out of the darkness as the River narrowed, shrinking from two and a half miles to barely half a mile, and I followed as it curved east. I rounded the bend, and suddenly found myself engulfed in downtown Jacksonville. Skyscrapers towered overhead. Logos and company names glowed brightly at their peaks, but most of their windows were still black. Both shores were awash in a chaos of lights, though I could detect no movement in the streets; the flaunting, flashing advertisements blazed out in vain onto an emptiness of dull concrete. The rich scent of coffee and baked goods came in thick on the breeze, mingled now and then with the sour hint of overfilled dumpsters. After over a week of simple living, the scale and intensity of everything was overwhelming, and I found that my heart was pounding anxiously. But the River seemed almost a matte black here, barely affected by the glimmer from the banks. It wove its way through the city dark and silent, and I was thankful to be veiled in it.

I passed several more bridges, following the River in an easterly direction for a couple of miles through the city center. I passed vast shipyards situated upon the banks of the north shore, harboring ships so massive that I seemed like a leaf floating on the water compared to their enormous bulk. Amidst the deeply contrasted light and shadow of scrap pieces littering the shore I heard the faint sound of welding torches, accompanied occasionally by the echoed clanking of hammers on metal. Gone were the peaceful, whispering forests that I had grown accustomed to; now a cold and lifeless shore glared at me in the dim grey of the approaching sunrise.

The River finally righted itself to a northerly heading again, and I stopped for a quick meal and some water under Mathews Bridge, the last bridge of the downtown area. For the first time I was able to clearly see the force of the current bubbling and swirling around its pylons. The tide was still coming in strong, but only about two hours more and that would change. As the first true light of dawn filled the sky, I struck back out and left the city behind me.

My surroundings changed quickly once I had left the heart of Jacksonville, but not back to forest. Instead, the shores became white sand, fluttering with sea oats and other hearty saltwater grasses. I noticed that even the air was beginning to smell salty as it swept by my face. No longer drab and dark, the River took on a new emerald hue as it sparkled in the morning sun.

I followed the northward stretch of the River for over four miles until it finally turned toward the ocean; from that point on it would hold a more or less easterly course until its waters met the Atlantic. Here the River ran to the north of Bartram and Quarantine Islands, and ahead in the distance was the Dames Point Bridge, the very last bridge of the entire trip, glinting pure white and arching a spectacular one hundred and seventy-five feet over the River. From calculations I had worked out previously, I knew that a shortcut through Mill Cove on the south side of the islands would save me half a mile, and the crystal blue waters seemed so calm that I decided to take it. I left the sandy shore behind me and headed out into the wide waters of the cove, feeling more certain than ever that I was as good as finished—I should have known better.

The wind grew quickly as if suddenly awakened by the bright, cloudless morning, and restless chop began forming on the surface of the water. I kept my sights on the Dames Point Bridge towering in the east. It seemed so close, and yet even after a good while of fighting those wind-swept waters, despite all my efforts, the bridge didn't seem to get any closer. I pushed hard for another stretch, but still it was no closer. Then I went on for what seemed like an hour, purposefully not glancing up until there was no doubt in my mind that I had made some good progress, yet even then it still looked the same as when I had started. I felt my will floundering. After all the distance I had covered and all I had been through, for some reason I was falling apart on this little four-mile run.

I was beginning to fade when suddenly there was a burst of air to my immediate right. I turned to look, but only caught a disturbance on the water. The burst of air then sounded behind me, and that time I thought I saw something just before it went under, though I wasn't sure. There was calm for a few moments, and then a dark figure suddenly broke the surface on my left—a dolphin! Another surfaced a little ways ahead of me, its dorsal fin almost black against the tossing blue waves. Then another appeared, then another—a whole pod was playing around the boat!

I instantly forgot my weariness and followed after them. The dolphins could have easily left me in their wake in moments, but instead they stayed with me as I paddled, surfacing and submerging around me in turn. I could see them darting through the sunlit water below, and above the noise of the wind I could even hear whistles and clicks as they called back and forth to one another. I wondered what they were saying—probably joking about my pathetic pace as I went awkwardly after them. One smaller juvenile was particularly curious of me, coming in so close that a couple of times I almost hit him unintentionally with my paddle, but he was quick enough to dodge out of the way. Before my blade hit the water he would vanish, only to resurface on the other side, rolling sideways and eyeing me playfully. Once he came up so close to me that I was sprayed with a fine briny mist as he exhaled.

I sputtered at the thick smell of old fish, but couldn't help laughing. "Brush your teeth, for crying out loud!"

They moved like missiles through the sparkling turquoise of the cove, shafts of refracted sunlight dancing wildly on their sleek bodies. I felt embarrassingly clumsy as I watched, mesmerized by their elegance and speed. They flashed by again and again, hurried and yet somehow coordinated with one another, as if they were performing an intricate dance they had long ago learned by heart.

Suddenly we were engulfed in shadow. A cloud? I looked up and was shocked to see the Dames Point Bridge looming over me. I had made it! I had no idea how long I had been paddling; my preoccupation with my new friends had made me completely forget about the task at hand! As if sensing that their work was done, the pod finally picked up speed and passed me by. I watched them go with amazement and gratitude, waving goodbye to them in spite of myself, then secured the boat behind the shelter of one of the pylons to get a well-deserved bite to eat.

After the Dames Point, Mill Cove reconnected with the main channel of the River, which was now barely a quarter mile wide. The wind was much calmer there, and the tide had finally turned, so I was able to cover the next five miles with relative ease. My progress was so good, in fact, that I began thinking about taking one last long break before I reached my goal, and before long I spotted a beautiful strip of white sand along the water's edge that made up my mind. My feet sank a bit as I stepped out into the shallows, and a few pale ghost crabs scuttled back to their burrows as I sloshed up. I ate a snack from my bag, took a swig of water, then with a contented sigh lay back on the sand with my hands behind my head.

A few gulls were squabbling with each other above me, wings stretched wide like sails, hovering in the coastal breeze. Thin white clouds soared even higher, inching lazily across the azure sky. A small patch of sea oats scratched against each other softly by a twisted piece of golden driftwood. I was still for a good while, taking it all in, then found myself thinking back on the many triumphs and near disasters that had marked my journey. I listened to the hush of the gentle waves, and thought about how the same water that was coursing by my feet had begun where I had, taking the same long, slow voyage from the swamp to the sea. We had both come a long way, the River and I, and now here we were at the end.

I finally forced myself to my feet once more and took in a deep breath of sharp, salty air. I dragged Old Orange back down to the water's edge—now a bit farther as the tide continued to ebb—and walked out until I was about shin-deep before jumping in and taking up my paddle. It was time for the final stretch.

As I left the shore, I noticed that the wind had picked up considerably. The surface of the River quickly grew into a crazed chaos of waves rushing from all directions, and it was difficult to hold my course. They smashed into me on all sides, drenching me within minutes and dumping a good deal of water into Old Orange in the process. I plowed my way east, knowing that no degree of skill could possibly keep me dry. When the waves grew even fiercer I hesitated for a moment, then hardened my resolve—I wasn't going to stop now. That northeast wind had been dogging me for the last five days, and it was not going to have the last word.

I raised my paddle in defiance into the salty blast. "You're still not gonna give up, are you, even when I'm this close? You wanna go one more round? Well, come on then! Let's go, you and me!"

I struck out with renewed strength, and the wind matched me in fury. "Come on!" I screamed at the gale, "Is that it? Show me what you've got! Stop me in my tracks!" A wave struck me broadside and the spray stung against my face, but I didn't care anymore. I could taste the salt—I was close. "Give it up!" I shouted as I thrashed against the waves. Another blast roared over the water in protest, sweeping up the surface in a fine mist and hunks of foam. "Give it up!" I shouted again. "You can't hold me back! I'll outlast you!"

I followed a slight bend in the River and suddenly, with one last long howl, the wind finally exhausted itself, and a still peace returned. Within minutes, the waters had gratefully calmed back to a sparkling teal, and as the ringing of the clamor faded from my ears I noticed the faint sound of deep, rhythmic booming. Just up ahead the River turned directly east, and as I cleared the bend, the two shores of the River fell away ahead of me for the last time, opening into a vast infinity of sparkling, rolling blue—the Atlantic. I couldn't believe it.

In nine days I had paddled three hundred and ten miles, from the St. John's humble birthplace in secluded wilderness to the wind-swept coasts where its waters mingled with the ocean. For nine days I had lived in sync with its rhythm, beat with its pulse, experienced both its beauty and its fury. I had traveled that River for years, but now I knew it in a way I never had before; thousands of sights and smells and emotions all melted together in my mind. Dark swamps silently alive with the ghost lights of timid fireflies; sandy pine scrubs burnished under a fierce noonday glare; mossy oak hammocks rocking in the damp gale of a coming storm; narrow passes, tempestuous lakes, shallow sloughs, vast expanses—it was all one complete whole.

For a short, fleeting breath of time, I had been privileged to travel through as a witness to its wonders, but I could never say that I conquered it. I had merely been a guest, a momentary ripple on its ancient surface. The River itself stopped for no one, relented for no one, and would never reveal all its secrets. If there had been any conquest, it was of the River over me, for even as I write this so many years after my journey, the desire to return still pulls at me, and my heart still races at the thought. When I run my hands through its dark, quiet waters, it's like the touch of an old friend, like waking the coursing stream of my own memory. Perhaps I gave so much of myself out there that I was never able to fully take it back. I had contended against all odds, against all fears, and had been forever changed, as all must be who would take that long journey, through dark and day, and at last reach the final shore at River's end.

Made in the USA
Columbia, SC
28 October 2024

44861822R10093